GREAT AMERICAN BATTLES

In this clear, dramatic review of America's major wars, Robert Leckie highlights eleven important battles. They range from James Wolfe's bold capture of Quebec and George Washington's surprise victory at Trenton to Douglas MacArthur's brilliant Korean War strategy at Pusan-Inchon.

Also included are the battles of New Orleans, Mexico City, Chancellorsville, Appomattox, Santiago, Belleau Wood, Guadalcanal, and D-Day.

GREAT AMERICAN BATTLES

by
ROBERT LECKIE

illustrated with maps,
prints and photographs

RANDOM HOUSE · NEW YORK

To the Glennon boys—
*Joe, Jimmy, Johnny, Tommy the Turk
and my godson Kerry*

ILLUSTRATION CREDITS: Bettman Archive: front endpaper, title page, 4, 7, 16, 19, 44, 45, 56–57, 63, 65 (left), 78, 89, 91, 98 (both); Bucks County Historical Society: 25; Culver Pictures: 20, 32, 37, 42–43, 48, 49, 51, 60, 72, 79, 96, 150–51, back endpaper; Defense Department: 58; Historical Pictures Service: 6, 8–9, 11, 21, 35, 54, 65 (right), 74, 77, 82, 84, 92, 95, 100, 102, 109, 114–15; Library of Congress: 14, 26, 86; Princeton University Library: 38, 53, 68, 71; The Smithsonian Institute: 112; United Nations: 158; United Press International: 105, 141, 146, 164, 169, 171; U.S. Army: facing Foreword, 144, 149, 153, 154, 161; U.S. Marines: 122, 126–27, 133, 137, 170, 172; U.S. Navy: 119, 131; U.S. Signal Corps: 1, 111; Wide World Photos: cover, 106, 128, 134, 162; Yale University Art Gallery: 28–29.

The map on page 67 is reprinted by permission of Random House, Inc., from *The Civil War: A Narrative,* Vol. II, by Shelby Foote (© Copyright, 1963, by Shelby Foote). The map on page 41 is reprinted by permission of The Bobbs-Merrill Company, Inc., from *The Life of Andrew Jackson* by Marquis James (Copyright, 1938, by Marquis James).

The maps on pages 81, 108, and 167 are by Harry Chester. The map on page 143 is by Jerome Kuhl.

Design, chapter-opening drawings, and the map on page 23 are by Theodore Cooper Burwell.

Some of the material in this book first appeared, in different form, in *The Wars of America* by Robert Leckie (Harper & Row, 1968).

Contents

Foreword

This book has two objectives. First, it attempts to present what may be called a capsule history of the wars of America. (The struggle still continuing in Vietnam is not included.) In so doing, it tries to explain not only *why* Americans went to war but *how* they went to war. It describes the weapons and tactics with which they fought, as well as the various methods they employed to raise armies.

The book's second purpose is to demonstrate the different ways in which a battle may be great. A battle is not to be measured by the number of men and arms engaged or the extent of casualties. A battle is great in how it changes the course of a war, how it affects history. Only a handful fell at Quebec, a "battle" that was actually just a sharp, half-hour's clash between armies of a few thousand men apiece. Yet it conquered a continent for Britain and changed Canada from a French into a British colony.

Who would compare Trenton to Saratoga, the most decisive battle of the Revolution? As battles go, Trenton was no more than a raid; yet it rescued George Washington's failing military reputation, saved his army, and rallied the Revolution. Without Saratoga there would have been no Yorktown; but without Trenton there would have been no Saratoga.

New Orleans suggests another way in which a battle may be great. For this engagement, fought after the war was over, nevertheless shows how the energy and will of a single commander such as Andrew Jackson may dominate a battlefield. Coming at the end of a long trail of military disgrace during the War of 1812, New Orleans also lets Americans believe they were never worsted in a war.

"To the victors belong the spoils," it is said, and no battle in history has produced greater booty than the fighting march on Mexico City. To undo the effects of that little victory would require the United States to restore to Mexico the modern states of California, Texas (probably), Nevada, Utah, Arizona, New Mexico, and parts of Wyoming and Colorado.

The inclusion of Chancellorsville may puzzle some readers. But it is the best illustration of the splendid command collaboration existing between Robert E. Lee and Stonewall Jackson. Lee to plan, Jackson to execute—that was the military team that terrified the North. A similar relationship existed between Grant and Sheridan. The series of movements lumped together under the name of Appomattox also stands as the conclusive battle of the Civil War.

Santiago is one of the few battles in which action on land led to action at sea. Usually the sequence is the other way around. Santiago also finished Spain as a first-class power and made America a two-ocean colossus while embarking her upon her international career.

Belleau Wood? Compared to such dreadful bloodbaths as Verdun, Belleau Wood was a tiny dogfight indeed. Yet, it not only saved Paris, but also impressed the Germans with American fighting qualities, while lifting the hearts of the war-weary Anglo-French. So small a struggle can do so much.

Guadalcanal was the perfection of all-or-nothing battle. Land, sea and air, it was a free-for-all—if one may speak so lightly of men suffering and dying. More important, Guadalcanal turned the tide of war against Japan. So also did Normandy sound the death knell of Nazi Germany. In a single day Normandy drastically altered the history of Western civilization. And D-Day was made possible by Eisenhower's decision to risk the greatest invasion force ever collected on the likelihood of finding a "hole in the storm."

Finally, Pusan-Inchon in Korea. These two related battles are splendid examples of the "delaying action" and the "deep envelopment." At Pusan, Americans traded space and blood for the time in which to gather forces for the decisive blow in the enemy's rear at Inchon. Douglas MacArthur used his army like a boxer blocking his opponent's Sunday punch with his left arm before launching the knockout blow with his right. When he did, he broke the North Koreans in two.

These, then, are the eleven battles chosen from all of America's wars save the struggle in Vietnam. As such, they are representative of a heritage of military success which is now, whether we like it or not, unrivaled in world history.

ROBERT LECKIE

Mountain Lakes, New Jersey
April 22, 1968

GREAT AMERICAN BATTLES

QUEBEC
Wolfe and Montcalm
Duel for a
Continent

At two o'clock in the morning of September 13, 1759, the tide of the mighty St. Lawrence River began to ebb past the French fortress city of Quebec. Upriver, where a British invasion fleet had gathered, a lantern with its light shrouded from the Quebec shore was hoisted to the main topgallant masthead of the *Sutherland*. It was the signal for boats full of British soldiers to cast off. One by one the boats silently slipped away from their mother ships.

In one of the leading boats stood General James Wolfe. Suddenly he began to speak in a low voice. He was reciting Gray's "Elegy in a Country Churchyard," which he had only just memorized. His aides listened quietly. Wolfe finished and said softly: "Gentlemen, I would rather have written those lines than take Quebec." An embarrassed silence ensued. No one believed the general. Wolfe said no more. Perhaps he was reflecting on one line of the poem:

3

"The paths of glory lead but to the grave."

Britain had planned her expedition to Quebec to be the knockout blow in the long Anglo-French struggle for possession of most of North America. That bitter conflict had been raging for 150 years. It had begun after Quebec was founded in 1609 and the first of the rival British colonies were established a few years later. It was part of a world-wide struggle for colonial supremacy. Each time a war broke out in Europe between the French and the British and their allies, its backlash would set the war fires blazing on the border between New France (as Canada was often called) and New England and New York. King William's War, Queen Anne's, King George's, all these had been fought between the rival colonies as part of the greater Anglo-French contest. In 1756 the final round (later known as the Seven Years' War) began. In America it was called the French and Indian War.

At first the French were everywhere

General Wolfe

successful. They held the Mississippi, penetrated New York and dominated what is now western Pennsylvania. Gradually, however, the British drove them back. By 1759 the French held only Fort Ticonderoga and Crown Point on Lake Champlain, in addition to their Canadian settlements along the St. Lawrence River.

To destroy these last French strongholds in the northern part of the continent, the British prepared two expeditions. One, under General Lord Jeffrey Amherst, was to clear Lake Champlain. The other was to take Quebec. Of the two, the Quebec operation was by far the more important. Quebec was the key to the St. Lawrence River, and the St. Lawrence was the key to all Canada.

When it was announced that this vital expedition was to be led by the 32-year-old James Wolfe, many older, more experienced generals were outraged. King George II was told that the youthful general was not only an upstart but also a madman. "Mad is he?" the old king growled. "Then I hope he bites some of my other generals."

In truth, James Wolfe did look a little odd. Tall and awkward, with long tapering fingers that seemed to pick constantly at his cuffs and buttons, he did not wear the military wig of a regular officer. He let his bright red hair grow long, pinning it at the back of his head like any jackanapes. But the nervous, foppish-looking Wolfe was actually a brave and

daring man. Moreover, he knew his profession, having been a soldier since the age of 14.

In those days the foot soldier carried a musket fitted at its muzzle with a long, slender bayonet. The musket itself was highly inaccurate, hard to load and had a killing range of only a hundred yards. So the bayonet usually determined the outcome of battle. In most of the engagements fought between the small, professional armies of the day, there was often only time enough for the attackers to deliver a single volley of musket fire. Then, under cover of the smoke from their guns, they would charge with the bayonet. The intent, of course, was to break the enemy's will and to put him to flight.

To employ or to resist such tactics required an iron discipline among the foot troops, while the involved drill used to move bodies of men about the battlefield also demanded extensive training. General James Wolfe was both a disciplinarian and an expert drillmaster. When he brought his little army of 8,500 men up the St. Lawrence in June of 1759, he was quite confident that he could conquer the fortress city of Quebec.

On June 26 his fleet anchored underneath the walls of the city. Next day his soldiers—American Rangers as well as British regulars—began going ashore on the abandoned Island of Orléans across the water from Quebec.

The defense of Canada was in the

5

General Montcalm

hands of Louis Joseph, Marquis de Montcalm-Gozon de Saint Véran. This small man with the long name was probably the most able soldier to come to the New World from France. Montcalm was scholarly, handsome and devoted to Church, king and family.

The general was subordinate to Pierre François de Rigaud, Marquis de Vaudreuil, the governor of Canada. Friendly and well-meaning, Vaudreuil was also vain and ambitious. He was jealous of Montcalm. By the summer of 1759 the Marquis de Montcalm and the Marquis de Vaudreuil had learned to distrust and despise one another.

Vaudreuil pretended that Montcalm's military victories were won by him, and Montcalm was disgusted by Vaudreuil's tolerance of a thieving *intendant* named François Bigot.

An intendant was a French official in charge of trade and finance. He also kept the army supplied. Almost all of the intendants of New France abused the office, using it for personal profit. Bigot, the most able of intendants, was also the most corrupt. His friendship with Vaudreuil sharpened Montcalm's distrust of the governor. That feeling turned to one of contempt after the British fleet arrived and Vaudreuil

6

attempted to destroy it with his "fire fleet."

The fleet was composed of fire ships —rotten old vessels soaked in pitch and tar and stuffed with bombs, grenades, old iron, fireworks, and rusty old cannon and muskets loaded to the muzzles. When lighted, they would drift down on the British fleet like floating volcanoes. The night of June 28, under a dark, moonless sky, the fire ships went up with a roar. To some of General Wolfe's sentries on the Island of Orléans, it seemed as though the world had exploded. Actually, the French sailors had applied their torches too soon. Before the fire ships could reach the British fleet, British sailors jumped into their boats, rowed boldly alongside the blazing hulks,

took them in tow and beached them. After the failure of the fire ships, Montcalm decided to rely strictly on himself and his troops.

In all, Montcalm had about 16,000 men—French regulars, Canadian militia and Indian allies. Because he considered Quebec's fortified walls to be impregnable, he left only 2,000 men holding the town and moved out to open ground on the east. Here was the one place at which Wolfe might be able to get around to the city's rear, and here Montcalm built a line seven miles long.

To the west of Quebec were high, steep cliffs which were impossible to climb. Even James Wolfe had to admit this when he examined the defenses of the city. Standing on a hill on the Is-

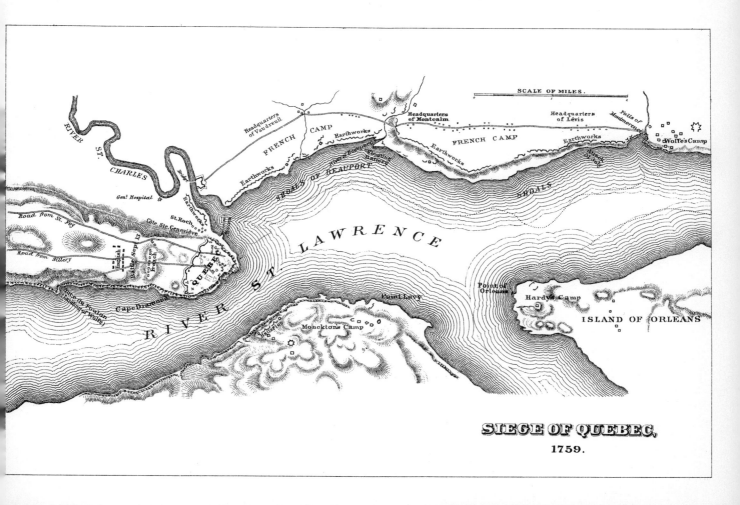

SIEGE OF QUEBEC, 1759.

land of Orléans, he studied the opposite shore through a telescope and found to his dismay that there did not seem to be any place to land.

Instead, he decided to bring Quebec under bombardment. Artillery was set up on the southern shore. By the middle of July, Wolfe's guns had begun the cannonade that eventually destroyed much of Quebec and forced many of its inhabitants to flee to the countryside.

General Montcalm, however, was not alarmed. He did not fear General Wolfe's forces as much as he feared the other army under General Amherst then advancing on Ticonderoga and Crown Point. If the French forts on Lake Champlain fell, the British would be able to attack Montreal to the west of Quebec. Montreal was the source of Montcalm's supplies. If it surrendered, Quebec would be cut off and could be starved into submission.

So Montcalm was undismayed by the British artillery, or by Wolfe's maneuvers aimed at drawing him out of his fortifications and into open battle. The only event that disturbed Montcalm was the British fleet's repeated success in running the gantlet of Quebec's guns, starting in midsummer, and gathering a force of ships upriver. This, again, put his line of supply west to Montreal in danger. Still, he decided to hold fast.

General James Wolfe, however, had no such patience. Thwarted in his attempts to draw Montcalm into the open, he launched a frontal attack on

An eighteenth-century drawing of Quebec.

8

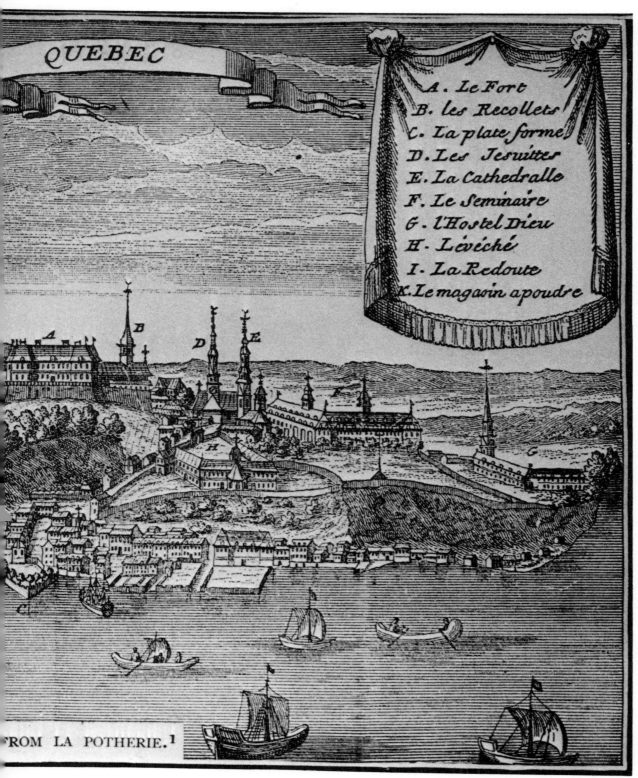

QUEBEC

A . Le Fort
B . les Recollets
C . La plate forme
D . Les Jesuittes
E . La Cathedralle
F . Le Seminaire
G . l'Hostel Dieu
H . L'évéché
I . La Redoute
K . Le magasin a poudre

FROM LA POTHERIE.[1]

Defenses of the walled town include the fort (A) and a redoubt (I).

the French line east of the city on July 31. The result was a sharp defeat in which Wolfe lost 443 men killed and wounded without harming a single Frenchman. He also lost the respect of almost all his staff officers. Even Vice-Admiral Charles Saunders, commander of the fleet, quarreled with the general.

Losing all patience, Wolfe ordered the countryside laid waste. East and west, British parties went forth to kill and burn. Night after night the residents of Quebec could see the glow of burning villages. Montcalm also witnessed this scourging of his countrymen, but he made no move to halt it. He knew that Wolfe was once again trying to draw him into open battle.

What the French commander still feared was an attack upon his rear by the British army under General Amherst. Amherst by then had taken Fort Ticonderoga and Crown Point. The way was open for him to descend Lake Champlain and fall on Montreal in Montcalm's rear.

But General Amherst dawdled at Ticonderoga until he could not possibly assault Montreal before the harsh, early Canadian winter ended all military operations. Montcalm felt safe. Gazing from his headquarters at the British across the river, he said: "Two months more, and they will be gone."

Toward the end of August it appeared that Montcalm was right. Wolfe's army was melting away. Since June he had lost more than 850 men

killed and wounded. Each day more men died of disease, or deserted to the enemy. Wolfe himself barely spoke to his three brigadiers: Robert Monckton, James Murray and George Townshend.

Then, on August 20, Wolfe fell seriously ill of a fever. He lay in the upper room of a French farmhouse, his frail body racked with pain. On the 25th, he began to recover. Four days later, he wrote to his brigadiers to ask them to "consult together to consider the best method to attack the enemy." Monckton, Murray and Townshend conferred. As they had done before, they advised Wolfe to seize the steep cliffs between Quebec and Montreal. Thus, he would cut the enemy's supply line and force upon Montcalm the choice between fighting or starving.

Wolfe agreed. His only concern now was to recover his health to lead such an operation.

"I know perfectly well you cannot cure me," he told his physician, "but pray make me up so that I may be without pain for a few days."

The three brigadiers were astounded. For months Wolfe had refused to take their advice to storm the cliffs to the west. Now he was proposing to capture the heights leading to the Plains of Abraham under the very nose of Quebec!

Historians still are not sure what caused James Wolfe to change his mind.

It has been said that Wolfe was on the edge of despair. He had told his

10

The effects of General Wolfe's bombardment of Quebec.

intimates that he would not go back defeated "to be exposed to the censure and reproach of an ignorant population." The very news that he could expect no help from General Amherst might have strengthened him in that resolution.

It has also been said that Wolfe was anxious to make one more attempt on the city before winter forced the fleet to depart. Soft thin floes of ice were already beginning to form in the Gulf of St. Lawrence. On September 10 Admiral Saunders assembled his officers and informed them that he thought the time had come to leave. Saunders had about 13,000 men under his command. With their ships they repre-

sented about a quarter of the strength of the British Navy. He could not risk being frozen into the St. Lawrence. All of Saunders' officers agreed, but Wolfe, upon being advised of this decision, rushed to Saunders' flagship and told him of his plan. He advised the admiral that he was going to send 150 picked men up a secret path to the Plains of Abraham. If they could overpower the light guard posted there, then his main body would follow. But if they could not, then Saunders could transport Wolfe and his soldiers back to England.

Wolfe is said to have seen this secret path while studying the heights west of Quebec. Examining a little cove called the Anse-du-Foulon, he is said to have spotted outlines of a path winding up the side of the supposedly inaccessible cliff. Then, observing that there were only a few tents pitched on the clifftop, he is supposed to have concluded that the guard there was light.

This is the generally accepted explanation of how James Wolfe discovered the chink in Montcalm's armor. It is also possible that an English engineer who had once been a French captive in Quebec knew of the path. Moreover, Wolfe had been active in interviewing enemy prisoners, and may have learned of the path from them.

Finally, it is possible that Quebec was betrayed. The scoundrel François Bigot and his thieving cronies may very well have wished the colony destroyed and all record of their dishonesty destroyed.

All that is known for sure is that Governor Vaudreuil, the protector of Bigot, countermanded Montcalm's orders—and left the Plains of Abraham unguarded. The crack Guienne Regiment under a capable colonel was moved from the Plains of Abraham back to the line of the St. Charles River.

Moreover, the guard of a hundred men which Montcalm had placed at the top of the Anse-du-Foulon was fatally crippled. It had been commanded by Captain St. Martin, a regular officer hand-picked for the duty by Montcalm. Vaudreuil replaced St. Martin with Duchambon de Vergor,

an officer who had been court-martialed for cowardice, and whom Bigot had once advised to "clip and cut" and rob the king. Where St. Martin had refused to allow the Canadians in his command to go home to help in the harvest, Vergor granted leave to 40 men on condition that they also put in a few hours of work on Vergor's own farm. Thus, the vital guard was already crippled.

Finally, the clifftops between the Anse-du-Foulon and Cape Rouge farther upstream were not even well patrolled on the night of Wolfe's attack. On that night the patrol commander could not use his three horses: one was stolen and two were lamed.

Thus, whether through accident or design, the key to Quebec was left unguarded on that fateful night of September 12–13, 1759, when red-headed James Wolfe made his final gamble for glory and a continent—or defeat and disgrace. On that night, the stars were visible but there was no moon as perhaps 4,800 English soldiers waited upriver in their ships.

Below Quebec, Admiral Saunders began lowering boats filled with sailors and Marines. He was making a "feint," trying to convince Montcalm that the attack was to come from another direction—ten miles below the Anse-du-Foulon.

It was then that the tide turned and began its downriver ebb.

It was then that the signal lantern was hoisted into view on *Sutherland's* masthead, that James Wolfe calmed his fears by quoting poetry—and that the British landing boats gathered speed on the outgoing St. Lawrence current.

Unchallenged and ignored, the boats glided downstream for two full hours. Now the tide was bearing the lead craft with Wolfe's spearhead —24 volunteers—toward the towering shore. Suddenly there was a shout in French.

"Who goes there?"

No one spoke, and then Simon Fraser, a young Highland officer who spoke French, shouted back:

"France! And long live the king!"

"What regiment?"

"The queen's," Fraser called back.

The sentry was satisfied and the boats drifted on, one of the men giggling aloud in relief. Again the challenge. A sentry had come scrambling down the cliff to stand at the water's edge and demand the password. Another French-speaking Highlander, Captain Donald MacDonald, gave the answer.

"Provision boats!" he replied, deliberately disguising his accent with a hoarse whisper. "Don't make such a bloody noise! The blasted English will hear!"

The sentry waved them on. The British could see the gray of his cuff against the black of the cliff behind him.

On the boats drifted. Now the current was running strong. Now they had rounded the headland of the Anse-du-Foulon. Breaking out their oars, the sailors rowed desperately against the tide. But the spearhead boats were swept too far downstream. Undaunted MacDonald, Fraser and their men leaped out. They found the secret path and climbed the cliff.

A French sentry shouted down at them. Still whispering hoarsely in French, MacDonald said that he had come to relieve the post. "I'll take care to give a good account of the English if they land!"

The sentry hesitated too long. Twenty-four shadowy figures rushed him before he could reply. Then the British charged with blazing muskets. Captain Vergor came dashing out of his tent, barefooted and nightshirted. He fired two pistols wildly into the air before he turned and ran. A musket shot struck his heel and he fell screaming.

It was then that James Wolfe waiting below heard the huzzahs of his triumphant volunteers. At once, he gave the order for the second wave to land. In came the boats, and soon the cliff face was crawling with British soldiers. Among them was James Wolfe. As he got to the top the empty boats of the first wave were returning to the packed transports for the rest of his troops.

By dawn, the last of Wolfe's sweating soldiers had struggled up to the undefended Plains of Abraham. Some 4,800 soldiers began to form a line less than a mile from the western walls of Quebec.

The British climbing Quebec's cliffs to the Plains of Abraham, as pictured in a London magazine a year later. The cliff was much higher and steeper than the artist realized, and the landing boats actually came from the other direction.

That was how the Marquis de Montcalm saw the British as he rode up in a drizzling rain.

Montcalm had been completely deceived by Admiral Saunders' feint. The French general had massed troops at the wrong place. Nevertheless, he rode back to Quebec that morning. Enroute, he learned of the British landing. Riding toward Vaudreuil's house he could clearly see the Plains of Abraham. Lines of British redcoats stretched from the St. Foye road on his right to the cliffs of St. Lawrence on his left. Faint on the wind, Montcalm could hear the skirl of Highland bagpipes.

"This is serious," Montcalm said to an aide.

He rode off to confer with his officers. Should he attack Wolfe immediately with the 4,000 troops on hand? Or should he wait for reinforcements?

His officers voted to attack at once. They did not wish to allow the British to dig in. They also feared that Vaudreuil might appear and issue more hamstringing orders. Montcalm agreed, and ordered his soldiers out to the Plains of Abraham.

Out the Palace Gate they poured

14

—the white-coated regulars of Old France, the buckskin-clad Canadians and painted Indians of the New World. With them rode their general. He was a splendid figure on his big bay horse. The Cross of St. Louis gleamed on the cuirass covering his green-and-gold uniform.

"Are you tired, my soldiers?" he called. "Are you ready, my boys?"

They answered him with cheers, and he waved his sword to encourage them.

Lying down to escape French artillery and sniper fire, the British awaited the French. James Wolfe strode among them. He wore a new uniform: scarlet coat, spotless white breeches and a silk-edged tricorne hat. He checked his men to be sure that they had loaded their muskets with an extra ball for the first volley. He paid no heed to enemy fire. When a captain near him fell, shot in the lung, Wolfe knelt and gently took the officer's head in his arms. The general thanked the captain for his service and promised him a promotion.

James Wolfe was elated. At last the all-or-nothing battle he had sought for so long had arrived. His step was light and his face shone. He was confident of victory, not because he outnumbered Montcalm by 4,800 to 4,000 troops, but because he had faith in his soldiers. He had trained them personally. He had taught them to hold their fire in awesome silence until the enemy was close enough to be shattered by a single volley.

At ten o'clock in the morning, the French began advancing down the slope from Quebec. Wolfe ordered his men to arise and form. On came the French, shouting loudly, firing as soon as they were within range. The British stood silent. Still the French approached, firing again. Now came the British command:

"Fire!"

The double-shotted British volley flashed out at the French not forty yards away. The French crumpled. Another British volley, and the field was obscured by smoke. When it lifted, the British saw the foe fleeing—and they charged with a cheer and the fierce wild yells of the Highlanders.

James Wolfe led the pursuit. He had already been wounded in the wrist and had wrapped a handkerchief around it. Now he was wounded again. When a third shot pierced his breast, he fell. Carried to the rear, he was asked if he wanted a surgeon.

"There's no need," he gasped. "It's all over with me."

He began to lose consciousness, until one of the sorrowing men around him shouted: "They run! See how they run!"

"Who run?" Wolfe cried.

"The enemy, sir. Egad, they give way everywhere!"

"Go one of you to Colonel Burton," Wolfe gasped, "and tell him to march Webb's regiment down to Charles River, to cut off their retreat from the bridge." Turning on his side, he murmured, "Now, God be praised, I will die in peace!" A few moments later he was dead.

The Marquis de Montcalm was also shot. Against his will his horse had been borne toward the town by the tide of fleeing French, and as he neared the walls a ball passed through his body. He slumped but kept his seat rather than let his soldiers see him fall. Two regulars bore him up on either side. He entered the city streaming blood in full view of two horrified women.

"Oh, my God!" one of them shrieked. "The marquis is killed."

"It is nothing, it is nothing," Montcalm replied. "Don't be troubled for me, my good friends."

But that night he was dying. His surgeon told him that his wound was mortal.

"I am glad of it," Montcalm said, and asked how much longer he had to live.

"Twelve hours, more or less," was the reply.

"So much the better," Montcalm murmured. "I am happy that I shall not live to see the surrender of Quebec."

Wolfe perished knowing that he

The death of Wolfe, painted about 1771 by the American-born British artist Benjamin West.

had won an important battle. Montcalm, dying, realized that his army was routed and demoralized.

Yet neither soldier realized how much was won and lost. The Battle of the Plains of Abraham turned out to be the crowning victory in the 150-year struggle for North America. By the Peace of Paris in 1763, France was stripped of all her American possessions except the Louisiana territory. Thus was concluded the chain of events set in motion by the handful of British volunteers who clambered up the slopes of the Anse-du-Foulon on the morning of September 13, 1759.

That night, as the victorious Wolfe lay dead, the governor of Quebec came to the defeated and dying Montcalm for instructions.

"I will neither give orders nor interfere any further," Montcalm replied. "I have much business that must be attended to, of greater moment than your ruined garrison and this wretched country. My time is very short, therefore pray leave me."

Comforted by the last sacraments of his church, courteous to the last, the Marquis de Montcalm died peacefully at four o'clock in the morning of September 14. His body was laid in a rough box nailed together by an aged servant of the Ursuline nuns. It was taken to the chapel of their shattered convent. Here a bursting shell had made a hole. Into this warrior's grave late that evening, by the flickering light of torches, the body of the last great soldier of New France was laid.

Two months later the *Royal William* sailed into Portsmouth in England carrying the coffin of James Wolfe. Guns were fired at minute intervals, muffled church bells tolled, flags were flown at half-mast and an escort stood on the dock with reversed arms. The route of the cortege from Portsmouth to London was lined with silent mourners, many of whom wept as they gazed upon the young general's bier. On November 20 "the corpse of General Wolfe was interred in a private manner in the family vault at Greenwich."

The man who conquered a continent had come home to rest, while the man who lost it had been buried where he fell.

TRENTON
Washington
Rallies the
Revolution

The English colonies were in open rebellion, and Parliament voted to raise an army of 55,000 men to crush them.

King George III heartily approved. The king was enraged by the "ingratitude" of the colonies. Instead of being thankful for England's destruction of the French enemy on their borders, instead of agreeing to help pay the costs of the French and Indian War, they had raised a ridiculous cry: "Taxation without representation is tyranny."

Even if they did insist that they were still loyal to the king, they had defied the king's ministers and his Parliament. Unfortunately for England, the long Anglo-French struggle had taught the colonies how to rule themselves. They thought that they had a "right" to self-rule, and they refused to pay any taxes which they themselves had not voted. So they resisted all of the taxes imposed by Parliament. After they had insulted the king by refusing

18

to buy British tea—even throwing it into the water of Boston Harbor—George III lifted the rod to chastise them.

The port of Boston was closed. General Thomas Gage was sent there to bring both that rebellious city and the disloyal colony of Massachusetts to their knees. In reply, the rebels began to gather arms. When Gage sent British regulars out to seize the arms, the rebels resisted in the Battle of Lexington-Concord. They fired on the king's soldiers—"the shot heard round the world." That was in April, 1775, and in that same year the American rebels fought British regulars at Bunker Hill.

Then came more outrages. The rebels seized one of the king's forts, at Ticonderoga on Lake Champlain. And the thirteen colonies elected a so-called "Congress" which fielded an upstart "army" under the command of a disloyal Virginia planter named George Washington.

It was then that Parliament voted to raise the force of 55,000 troops to crush the rebellion. However, the king's subjects did not rally to his cause. Many of his officers, sympathizing with the Americans, did not wish to serve against them. Few of his ordinary subjects were attracted to the poor pay and brutal discipline of British Army ranks. So King George of England went looking for hirelings. He found them in the little principalities of Germany: Brunswick, Waldeck, Anhalt-Zerbst, Anspach-Beyreuth, Hesse-Hanau, Hesse-Cassel. Eventually some 30,000 German mercenary soldiers were hired for the American war. More than half of

An early print of the Battle of Lexington.

them were supplied by the ruler of Hesse-Cassel, and they all came to be known as Hessians.

The colonies rocked with rage to learn that the king was sending the Hessians against them. True enough, it was then customary for a king to hire outside troops to fight his battles. But this was always against a *foreign* foe. The colonials still considered themselves George's loyal subjects. They were not fighting him, they insisted, only his stubborn ministers and high-handed Parliament. Now, he was treating them no better than the despised French and Spanish! Now, the colonials reasoned, there was nothing left to do but cut the last ties that bound them—and in July of 1776 they proclaimed their Declaration of Independence.

A Hessian soldier

A month later the Hessians began landing on Long Island.

Great white sails crowded Gravesend Bay. Boats filled with red-coated British regulars and Hessians in blue, scarlet and green uniforms were rowed toward shore. The bright sun made a million points of light on bayonets and burnished buckles, on flashing white oars and on the instruments of shipboard bands playing lively tunes. By noon 15,000 men had joined General William Howe in America, and three days later 5,000 more came ashore.

Between them, the British redcoats and the Hessian mercenaries began to sweep all before them.

They defeated General George Washington's troops in the Battle of Long Island. Here the Hessians went into battle singing hymns. They mercilessly bayoneted many of the ragged rebels who tried to surrender. The Hessians' excuse was that they had been told by the British that the Americans gave no quarter.

One of the Hessian officers who distinguished himself on Long Island was Colonel Johann Rall. He also fought brilliantly when General Howe nearly trapped the fleeing General Washington at White Plains. And it was Colonel Rall who later led the charge against Fort Washington on Manhattan Island.

"All you that are my grenadiers, march forwards!" he cried.

With that, drums began to beat, oboes blew and the music-loving Hes-

The last stand of the American rebels at the Battle of Long Island. Hessians in conical helmets can be seen attacking in the rear.

sians—awesome in their tall brass hats —swept forward to help compel the Americans to surrender.

The British and their Hessian allies were jubilant. They had beaten the rebels again and again. They were so contemptuous of American fighting prowess that one of the English officers swore he would travel the length of the colonies and force all the American men to put on petticoats. Colonel Rall agreed with him. In fact, even General Washington would find it

difficult to disagree, for his men had not been fighting too valiantly. Defeat and retreat—that had been his Continental Army's portion throughout the black summer and fall of 1776.

In November, Washington led his ragged remnant across the Hudson River and into New Jersey. General Howe sent Lord Cornwallis after him, and Washington began a miserable retreat across New Jersey into Pennsylvania. Again and again, he fired off instructions to General Charles Lee, who was farther north, to join him with the main body of American troops. Desertions were whittling down Washington's army. If Lee would only come, the combined force would number at least 10,000 men. But Lee did not, and Washington's force melted away to barely 3,000 soldiers.

Onward and onward Washington led his wretched scarecrows. Many of them were without shoes or stockings, and they suffered bitterly. Into Newark they trudged, and out of it; into New Brunswick, and away again to Trenton, with the eager Cornwallis snapping at their heels. Now they were on the Delaware River. Even as Congress prepared to flee from Philadelphia to Baltimore, General Washington began collecting boats. At last, Washington's army was across the river—safe in Pennsylvania.

Safe?

Safe to starve or to fall apart! In another few weeks enlistments in the Continental Army would expire and Washington despaired of obtaining new recruits. His supplies were low. If only General Lee would hurry south from New York . . . If he did not, Washington wrote to his cousin Lund Washington, "I think the game will be pretty well up."

A few days later, George Washington learned that the British had captured General Lee.

Many Americans were more dismayed by the capture of Charles Lee than by the defeats at Long Island, New York and White Plains. They believed that Lee, a professional soldier who had been born in England, was the superior of the "backwoodsman" Washington, whose only experience of war had been gained in frontier fighting against the French and their Indian allies. In those days, such hit-and-run skirmishing was scorned by the "professionals," military specialists to whom arms was a full-time career. These officers were skilled in the various "evolutions"—the movements of their highly trained troops from place to place on the battlefield. They also knew how to construct fortifications, how to use their artillery to rout the enemy or to support their own troops, how to compel a fort to surrender and how to keep their soldiers clothed, fed, sheltered and armed. These were the various arts of war which, becoming more and more specialized, required more and more expert knowledge and experience.

Because of this, an expert like Lee was considered by some people to be of much more value to the new nation than a so-called "amateur" like George Washington. Even Washington was crushed at Lee's capture, although he knew that Lee had been intriguing behind his back with General Horatio Gates, a veteran of the British Army who had become an American planter.

But then the blow was softened by the arrival of Lee's troops, who had eluded the British. Now George Washington was going to attack!

Attack? The beaten rebels turn on the victorious British? Who could believe that Washington would be so audacious? Certainly very few of the despairing Congressmen then gathering in Baltimore.

Yet Washington saw clearly that he *had* to attack. He could not wait until the Delaware froze and then became passable. He could not wait until the dying rebel cause breathed its last. No, he had to take counsel from the immortal rallying cry which had come from the pen of Tom Paine, and which the general had read to his troops: "These are the times that try men's souls. The summer soldier and the sunshine patriot will, in this crisis, shrink from the service of their country; but he that stands it now, deserves

the love and thanks of man and woman."

George Washington believed this. He was confident that if he could strike one strong blow against the overconfident enemy, he would restore his infant nation's faith in its destiny. Where, then, to strike?

Trenton.

Across the Delaware in New Jersey were 3,000 Hessian soldiers holding a six-mile line from Bordentown north to Trenton. Half of them were at Trenton under Colonel Johann Rall. Washington knew that the Hessians were in winter quarters and that they feared little harm from the Americans. Colonel Rall had already boasted that he could "keep the peace in New Jersey with a corporal's guard." He had

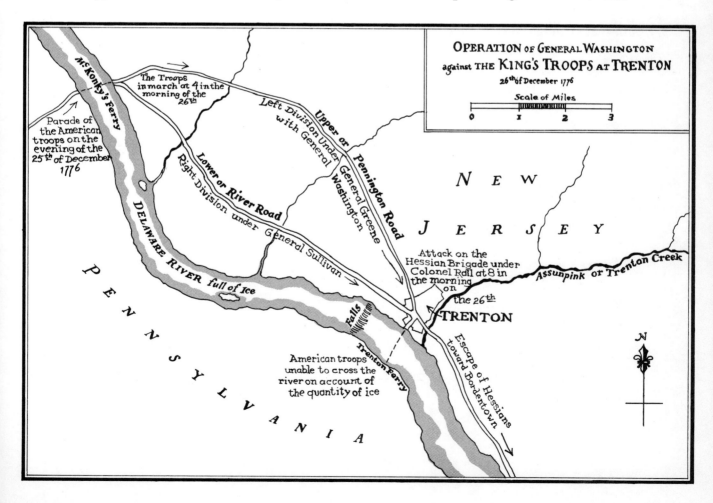

barely more than that posted to defend Trenton. If Washington could slip up on Rall and his Hessians unawares, he might bring off that brilliant counterstroke which he needed so badly.

So the general made his plans.

One force of about 2,000 men was to cross the Delaware downriver to engage the enemy force at Bordentown and prevent it from coming to Trenton's rescue.

A second force of 900 men would cross opposite Trenton to capture Assunpink Creek bridge below the town and thus seal off the escape route south to Bordentown.

The third, the main body of about 2,400 men, would be led by Washington himself. He would cross the Delaware above Trenton on Christmas night and march downstream to deliver his surprise attack on the town one hour before dawn.

On Christmas night, the ragged Continentals marched to McKonkey's Ferry, where Washington had collected his boats. A storm raged around them. Snow mixed with sleet blew into their faces. Even General Washington drew his cloak around him. Near the ferry Major James Wilkinson, the aide of the captured General Charles Lee, presented himself with a letter from General Horatio Gates. Washington was astounded to learn that Gates, his northern commander, was in the vicinity.

"From General Gates?" he asked. "Where is he?"

"I left him this morning in Philadelphia, sir."

"What was he doing *there?*"

"I understood him that he was on his way to Congress."

"On his way to Congress!" Washington repeated, shaken. Without permission General Gates, the intriguing confidant of General Charles Lee, had gone to Baltimore. What could he be up to among those disgruntled politicians? What would Gates and his Congressional friends make of another Washington defeat?

Now, more than ever before, the general must win at Trenton.

In Trenton that Christmas morning, Colonel Johann Rall had awakened with his customary fuzzy feeling from a night of eating and drinking. A fine fighter and a brave man, Colonel Rall was also a believer in having a good time away from the battlefield. So he arose and dressed, while shivering Hessian bandsmen serenaded him outside his window.

Colonel Rall paid little attention to the disposition of his troops throughout that Christmas day. He had not built redoubts around Trenton, as he had been ordered to do, and he had only a few pickets stationed along the roads.

That Christmas night, there was a slight alarm when a roving American patrol ran into a picket guard. The troops were called to arms. But then they were returned to quarters, and Colonel Rall went to a supper party at the home of a wealthy Trenton Tory. He played cards and drank wine.

Around midnight, there was a knock

George Washington preparing to cross the Delaware, painted by Edward Hicks, an American artist born during the Revolution.

on the door. A Tory was outside with information for Colonel Rall. The colonel refused to see him. The man then wrote a note warning Rall that the American Army was on the march. The note was delivered by a servant. Intent upon his game, Rall stuck it into his pocket unread.

At length Colonel Johann Rall returned home, his head heavy with wine. He went to bed. Outside his window, the storm howled higher.

Washington had ordered his men to keep silent. No soldier was to break ranks under pain of death. Standing by the landing, their heads ducked into their collars against the snowy sleet, they tried to keep their firelocks dry. But they became hopelessly wet. Fortunately, Colonel Henry Knox's artillerymen were able to keep their cannon touchholes dry.

Suddenly the order came to enter the boats. Then men stepped gingerly into their bobbing shells. They pushed off. Cakes of ice floating downstream struck the vessels so hard that it was difficult to keep them afloat. The crossing fell behind schedule. Washington had hoped to have his troops on the Jersey bank by midnight, but it was not until after three o'clock in the morning that Colonel Knox's deep bass voice was heard announcing that the crossing was completed.

Across the river Washington divided his little army of 2,400 men into two. One force under John Sullivan marched down the river road toward Trenton. The other under Nathanael Greene and accompanied by George Washington marched along a road two miles farther inland. This way, Sullivan would strike the bottom of the town, and Greene would hit the top.

In silence the crucial march began. Buffeted by the icy wind, the rebels slid and fell on the slippery roads. Cruel ice cut through their flimsy foot-gear and slashed their feet. In the morning, Major Wilkinson could follow the route by the bloodstains in the snow.

Undaunted, the rebels pushed on. Mile by mile they slipped up on the sleeping Hessian foe. Just at daylight both columns reached their destination. Both ran into Hessian pickets.

"Der fiend! Heraus! Heraus!" the pickets shouted. "The enemy! Turn out! Turn out!"

Lieutenant Jacob Piel heard the warnings and hurried to wake Colonel Rall. He pounded on the colonel's door. Rall, in his night clothes, poked his head out the window. Piel said that he had heard shouting. Rall ducked hastily back into his room and began to dress. A few minutes later he came rushing out of his building in

The rebels attack at Trenton.

full uniform. Issuing orders in German, he formed his own blue-coated regiment on King Street. The scarlet-coated Lossbergs marched to Rall's right to defend Queen Street, parallel with King. In the rear, the black-coated Knyphausen Regiment made up the reserve.

At the top of both King and Queen Streets stood the American artillery, two guns to a street. Would they fire? On King Street, Captain Alexander Hamilton's gunners blew on their slow matches. They stuck them in the touchholes...

Ba-loom! Ba-loom!

The cheers of the Americans mingled with the shrieks of the stricken Hessians. Grapeshot mowed down Rall's regiment like hay. His men fell back.

Now, on Queen Street, the other pair of American guns spoke. Mounting their own cannon, the Lossbergs fired back. The Americans charged them. Portly Captain William Washington and young Lieutenant James Monroe swung their swords and ran forward. Both were wounded, but their men pressed forward to capture the Hessian cannon.

Now there came the sound of firing at the bottom of the town. Sullivan's men were attacking from the west. Nathanael Greene's division extended its flank to join with Sullivan. Some of Greene's men worked around to the rear or east of the town. If Washington's second force had crossed the Delaware and held the Assunpink Creek bridge as planned, the Hessians would be trapped.

But the second force was not there. The bridge was open and as many as 400 Hessians were fleeing across it. But most of their comrades could not escape.

"Use the bayonet!" George Washington cried to his men. "I am determined to take Trenton!"

With their firelocks wet, bayonets were about all both sides could use. Sometimes, however, the Americans ducked inside the buildings to dry their pieces or pick the touchholes clear. Then they began sniping from the windows. Some of them aimed at Colonel Johann Rall, just as the mounted Hessian commander reformed his shattered troops and prepared to counterattack. The Americans fired and two bullets pierced Rall's body. He toppled from his horse, fatally wounded.

Now the Hessians were demoralized. Sullivan's men had seized the vital bridge and blocked the escape route. There was nothing left to do but surrender. One by one the Hessian regiments threw down their arms. In all, about 920 of them were taken prisoner, while 25 had been killed and 90 wounded. American losses were two men who froze to death on the march, and four others wounded. Not a single American had died at Trenton.

Casualties, of course, do not measure victories. Rather, victories are measured by the effect they have upon the entire war. Thus Trenton—no more than a raid in which little blood

"The Capture of the Hessians at Trenton" by John Trumbull (who served in the Continental Army as an aide to Washington). Colonel Rall, fatally wounded, is shown surrendering to Washington. James Monroe is lying wounded behind Rall. (Yale University Art Gallery)

was shed—was to have enormous consequences for the American Revolution. It lifted the Americans out of their deep despair and sent their spirits soaring high. It astounded Europe. France and Spain, delighted to hear that their archenemy, England, had been humbled by the rebels, began to think seriously of helping the Americans.

Trenton also stunned the English. Sir William Howe could not believe that "three old established regiments of a people who made war a profession should lay down their arms to a ragged and undisciplined militia."

Because of Trenton, Washington the "amateur" was hailed as a military genius. Intriguers like Horatio Gates ceased to conspire against him, and a grateful Congress voted him powers which made him a virtual military dictator. And, while battalions of militia rushed to join the victorious American general, Washington was able to persuade his regulars to re-enlist in the Continental Army. Thus, most important of all, by the daring military gamble at Trenton, George Washington saved his army.

Well might that tall commanding figure stand radiant on the field at Trenton in the daylight of December 26, 1776. When Major Wilkinson rode up to him to report that the last Hessian regiment had surrendered, Washington's face shone and he put out his hand in thanks.

"Major Wilkinson," he said, "this is a glorious day for our country."

NEW ORLEANS
Old Hickory
Holds Firm

At the end of the 1700s a great though despotic soldier came to power in France. His name was Napoleon Bonaparte. The series of bloody conflicts called the Napoleonic Wars were to be the indirect cause of the second war between Britain and America—the War of 1812.

Napoleon's ambition was to rule Europe. He was opposed by Britain and her allies. Britain proclaimed a blockade of Europe and announced her intention of capturing any ship that did not obey her blockade rules. Napoleon replied by closing European ports to British shipping and proclaiming *his* right to seize any ship that dealt with Britain. These actions had grievous consequences for the United States, for by the beginning of the 1800s the young American nation had a large fleet of merchant ships. Because America was neutral in the Napoleonic Wars, her ships were stopped at sea by *both* the French and the British.

The United States suffered more at the hands of Britain. This was because the British, unlike the French, sailed right up to the shores of America to enforce their blockade. Not only did they seize American ships, but they also impressed American seamen into service on their own vessels. Americans became enraged. As the Napoleonic Wars continued and the British Navy became more high-handed, the public outcry for another war with Britain became louder and louder.

It became loudest in 1811 when the War Hawks took control of Congress. These men were mostly from the American West and South, and some of them had never smelled salt water. Yet they were constantly thundering the slogan: "Free Trade and Sailors' Rights!"

The War Hawks' public protest against Britain's conduct on the ocean was a cover for their private motive— more land. They wanted the fertile woods of what is now the Province of Ontario in Canada, as well as more Indian lands in the Old Northwest. In truth, they did have a complaint against Canada as the source of British support of the Indians, then beginning to raid American settlements in the Old Northwest. But because so few people were affected by the Indian uprisings, the nation as a whole did not feel threatened.

What the War Hawks needed was a general grievance, and this was supplied when the sensitive young nation's feelings of "national honor" were outraged by British insults on the high seas. After the British blockade also caused a depression in the South and West, the War Hawks were able to persuade Congress to declare war on Britain. On June 18, 1812, President James Madison signed the declaration which began the War of 1812.

Never in American history has there been a conflict so useless and so humiliating. Its beginning was tragic: two days before President Madison signed the declaration of war, a new British government suspended the blockade orders. Thus, the United States went to war without a reason for war. If communications had been better, the War of 1812 might never have begun.

From tragedy the war went to travesty. There was only a tiny standing army. That was because the American people still regarded a large one as a threat to liberty. After the Revolution they had hastened to disband their armed forces. By 1802 the U.S. Army was down to 175 officers, 12 cadets and 2,389 enlisted men. It did little else but guard the frontier. When the War of 1812 came, the government made frantic attempts to enlarge the Army, but it was forced to rely mainly upon the state militia.

As in the Revolution, militia were bodies of citizen-soldiers much like the modern National Guard. They met monthly to drill and were called out only in emergencies. Being state organizations, they were subject to the orders

31

British sailors "impressing" an American.

of the state governors. In the War of 1812 half of the militia, especially those of New England, refused to serve. This was because the War of 1812 was not completely popular. Except for New York, Kentucky, Tennessee and perhaps Ohio—the regions most likely to benefit from a victory—no state gave the war its full support. New England actually became wealthy through trading with the enemy. In fact, New England was so opposed to the war that at one time it considered seceding from the Union.

On land, American arms were ingloriously defeated. All attempts to conquer Canada were roundly repulsed, and the city of Detroit was even surrendered to a British army. One or two minor successes were won along the border between New York and Ontario, but in the main the Ameri-

cans were so badly worsted that they could not even prevent the British from capturing Washington. President Madison and his cabinet and most of Congress fled, and the British set fire to the city.

On the water, however, American fortunes fared better. British nautical pride was badly bruised by the single-ship victories won by American frigates such as the famous *Constitution,* known as "Old Ironsides." The victory on Lake Erie, won by the youthful Commodore Oliver Hazard Perry, kept control of the Great Lakes in American hands. Perhaps even more important was the miniature naval Battle of Lake Champlain, won by the Americans under Lieutenant Thomas Macdonough. This triumph forced an overwhelmingly superior British invasion force to retreat from New York

State. It also shook the British government. The Prime Minister, Lord Liverpool, decided to talk peace.

Earlier, the British had been prepared to impose terms that would have reduced the United States to the status of a second-rate power on the Atlantic seaboard. Under the generalship of the great Duke of Wellington, the British and their allies had finally defeated Napoleon. Enraged at having been attacked by their American cousins when they stood in their greatest peril, the British resolved to humble the United States. The greatest invasion force ever mounted against a New World city was ordered to capture New Orleans. This would give Britain control of the mouth of the Mississippi River and deprive the American West of its outlet to the sea. Moreover, New Orleans would be a valuable prize in itself. So the ships carrying 10,000 British regulars—the conquerors of Napoleon—crowded on sail for the Gulf of Mexico. Commanding this force was Sir Edward Pakenham, the Duke of Wellington's brother-in-law.

After it departed, the British had their change of heart. The entire country had become war-weary, and the news of the defeat at Lake Champlain had been received. So it was that Britain was eager to end the war, and on Christmas Eve, 1814, the Treaty of Ghent was signed.

By then, however, it was too late to recall the armada bound for New Orleans. There was no radio or telegraph then, and no ship was fast enough to overtake the expeditionary force. So it sailed on. Waiting to oppose the 10,000 British regulars were a handful of American regulars and a few thousand militia, led by a lean Tennessee frontiersman named Andrew Jackson.

Shortly after the war broke out, Andrew Jackson had led his Tennessee militia on a march to reinforce New Orleans. But the general in charge, who was jealous of Jackson, refused to allow him to enter the city. So Jackson had to march his men home again. On that grueling journey, Jackson dined on acorns at least once. One of his men gazed admiringly at the lean, tireless figure leading them onward, and said, "He's tough—tough as hickory." And so the nickname "Old Hickory" was born.

However, that roundabout march seemed to be the beginning and end of Old Hickory's career as a general. As often as he volunteered for action on the northern battlefronts, he was rejected by the inept Secretary of War, John Armstrong. And then Old Hickory's hot temper very nearly ended his career.

In September, 1813, Jackson's enemies, Thomas and Jesse Benton, came into Nashville. Wearing two pistols apiece, the Benton brothers went to the City Hotel. Jackson followed, accompanied by his friend, the gigantic John Coffee. Both were armed, and Old Hickory carried a whip.

Spotting Thomas Benton in a doorway, he shook the whip and roared:

"Now, defend yourself, you damned rascal!"

Benton went for his pistol, but Jackson beat him to the draw. Pistol at his rival's breast, Old Hickory backed him step by step through a corridor. But then Jesse Benton stole up behind Jackson. Jesse drew and fired. Jackson tumbled forward, his own pistol discharging harmlessly, while blood spurted from his left side.

No one else was hurt, but Old Hickory had been gravely wounded. His doctors said that, if he did not let them amputate his arm, he would die.

"I'll keep my arm," Old Hickory muttered.

He lay in agony in his bed in the Hermitage, as he called his home. There he learned that the Creek Indians were on the warpath.

His arm in a sling, his thin face white with pain, Jackson put himself at the head of his little army to defeat the Creeks in a brilliant wilderness campaign. As a result, 23 million acres—comprising three-fifths of Alabama and one-fifth of Georgia—were ceded to the United States. Old Hickory's reputation was made. But Secretary of War Armstrong was still jealous of him. It was not until after Armstrong was dismissed and the nation was on the brink of disaster that Andrew Jackson was called upon to defend New Orleans.

At first, Old Hickory was confident that the British invasion force would attack Mobile in Alabama before moving against New Orleans. Because the great Louisiana city would be easy to defend, Jackson believed that the enemy would move from Mobile to the area above the city. Holding the Mississippi, the British could cut New Orleans' supply line and starve the city into submission.

However, Old Hickory had not reckoned on the lust for prize money which dwelt in the heart of Admiral Sir Alexander Cochrane, the British naval commander. Admiral Cochrane was on the island of Jamaica with his fleet, waiting for the arrival of Sir Edward Pakenham. The admiral knew that the wharves in New Orleans were piled high with millions of dollars' worth of produce from the American West. In those days, an officer was allowed to make a personal profit from captured stores. So Cochrane decided not to wait for Sir Edward. With Major General John Keane in charge of the troops, he sailed for New Orleans.

As he did, General Jackson also decided to head for the city. He sent big John Coffee on ahead to Baton Rouge with 2,000 mounted riflemen. Then he followed with another 2,000 foot soldiers. On December 1, 1814, Old Hickory reached the outskirts of New Orleans.

To some who awaited him there, his appearance was not impressive. He looked unhealthy. His face was sallow, and his short blue Spanish cloak hung loosely on his thin body. There was mud on his boots. His iron-gray hair beneath his little leather cap was

Andrew Jackson during the Creek Wars, convincing the militia at gunpoint that their enlistments are not yet up. His arm is still in a sling from his fight with the Benton brothers.

matted and unkempt. To one fine lady of French extraction, Old Hickory was just "an ugly old Kaintuck flatboatman." Yet, another observer thought that the most compelling feature of Jackson's appearance was "the fierce glare" that lighted "his bright and hawk-like eye."

Next day General Jackson entered New Orleans itself. Almost at once he impressed its populace, who were mostly French. He began strengthening the forts protecting the city. The numerous bayous or canals were blocked by felled trees, and troops were placed in position to cover each of these bayou blocks.

Then Jackson put on a new uniform, swung aboard a splendid mount and rode off to review his troops.

It was a colorful parade. Regulars in regulation blue mingled with militia in gray, with Creoles wearing the baggy red pants of French zouaves, with free Negroes in homespun, with painted Choctaw Indians. There were also fierce, red-shirted pirates from nearby Barataria, with curled mustaches and dangling earrings. The pirates were commanded by Jean Lafitte. At first, Jackson called them "hellish banditti" and spurned Lafitte's offer of service. But then the pirate captain confronted Old Hickory in his headquarters, looked him boldly in the eye and convinced the general that the Baratarians, after all, "could not fail of being very useful."

Two days after the review, John Coffee's dragoons clattered into town from their outpost at Baton Rouge. A few hours later 3,000 Tennessee volunteers under William Carroll came bobbing down the Mississippi on flatboats. Now Jackson wrote home to his beloved wife, Rachel: "All well."

Even after the British fleet sailed into Lake Borgne—the watery link between the Gulf of Mexico and the left bank of the river below New Orleans—the general was not worried. He sat tight while the enemy captured five gunboats on the lake. He did not move because he was still confident that every bayou between Borgne and the riverbank was blocked and guarded.

On December 23, 1814, Jackson was in his headquarters. There was a clatter of horse's hoofs outside the window. His door flew open and a young officer ran in to announce the arrival of three gentleman with "important intelligence." The trio rushed in, breathless and mud-stained. Major Gabriel Villere burst into a torrent of French. The astounded Jackson heard an interpreter explain that the British had landed on the western shore of Lake Borgne and had captured the Villere family's plantation. Jackson could hardly believe that the enemy had found an unguarded bayou and had passed through a swamp and were now on the river only seven miles below New Orleans. But then his eyes flashed and he sprang from his sofa.

"By the Eternal," he cried, "they shall not sleep on our soil!"

Growing calm again, he ordered

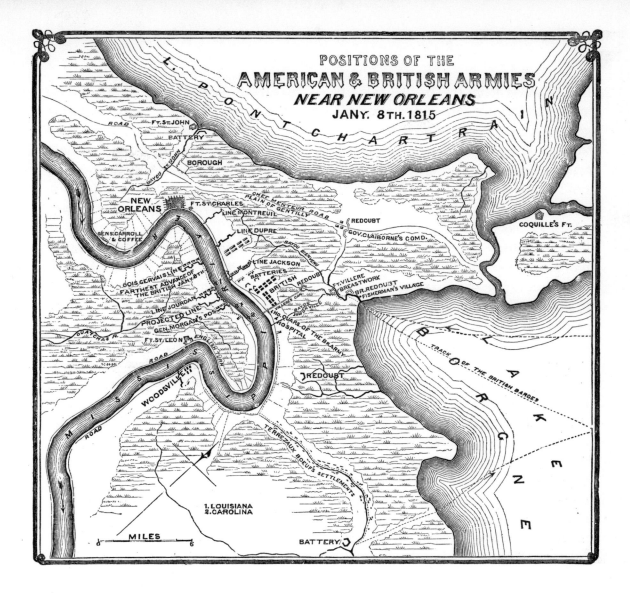

POSITIONS OF THE
AMERICAN & BRITISH ARMIES
NEAR NEW ORLEANS
JANY. 8TH. 1815

wine for his visitors and called a conference among his officers.

"Gentlemen," he told them, "the British are below. We must fight them tonight."

Old Hickory could spare about 2,000 men for his night assault. He also had the schooner *Carolina,* riding low in the water under the weight of Jean Lafitte's guns and gunners. At dusk *Carolina* began slipping downstream toward Villere Plantation on the left. There the British had built fires, which blazed cheerfully in the darkness. They proved inviting targets for *Carolina.*

Aboard the schooner, Captain Daniel Patterson prepared to open fire at 7:30 P.M. A half-hour later, time enough for the enemy to conclude that American troops were striking from the river, Jackson would attack down the riverbank.

Now a cold fog rose from the Mississippi. Mist dimmed the moon and hid *Carolina* from the British soldiers at Villere. Suddenly the schooner's guns began bellowing. Red blobs sailed through the fog. Shells smashed and crashed among the startled British. For a moment, they were close to panic. But then the iron discipline which had conquered Napoleon took hold. Bonfires were put out and the redcoats scrambled for the cover of the Mississippi levee. *Carolina* continued the bombardment.

At exactly eight o'clock, Jackson's men attacked on land.

They charged behind a barrage from their six-pounders. As *Carolina* fell silent, fearing to fire on friend and foe alike, the British turned to fight. At once, the battle became a confused, blind blunder in the misty dark. Neither General Jackson nor General Keane could exercise much control. It was simply squad for squad, man for man. Soldiers groped for each other in the darkness or fired at targets outlined by cannon muzzles gushing flame. At one point, the British tried to capture the American six-pounders.

"Save the guns!" Old Hickory roared. A body of Marines and soldiers rallied around him to beat back the British.

At midnight General Jackson called off his attack. He had guessed that General Keane was bringing up more troops and would soon outnumber him.

Nevertheless he had dealt the British a serious blow. They had been confident that the "Dirty Shirts," as they called Jackson's men, would run from the regulars. But they had not. In fact, they had been first to attack and had suffered only half as many casualties. Satisfied, Old Hickory stationed his men behind the dry Rodriguez Canal two miles upriver from the British position, and ordered them to dig in.

General Jackson supervises his troops during the night battle near Villere Plantation.

It was on December 24, 1814, that the Treaty of Ghent "ended" the War of 1812. But it would be weeks before the Americans and British at New Orleans learned of it. So Christmas Day there began with a salvo of British artillery. The Americans building mud ramparts behind the canal dropped their shovels and seized their muskets. But there was no enemy attack. The British had merely fired a salute to Sir Edward Pakenham, who had arrived to take command from General Keane.

Pakenham's presence lifted the British Army's drooping spirits. The redcoats were fond of the boyish hero of Salamanca, the battle in which Wellington had crushed the French armies in Spain. Pakenham was himself eager for victory. If he won, he would become an earl and be made royal governor of Louisiana. His wife was at sea, awaiting the news of that happy event. So were many other British subjects, all of whom were prepared to take over the administration of New Orleans. Here, of course, was proof that the British Crown intended to hold on to the great city at the mouth of the Mississippi.

To take it, Sir Edward proposed to withdraw from his army's present poor position and land elsewhere. But his mind was changed by Admiral Cochrane.

Scornful of the Dirty Shirts, this bluff old sea dog swore that his sailors alone could beat Jackson. "The soldiers could then bring up the baggage," he sneered.

Pakenham was stung. He unwisely agreed to storm Jackson's fortifications.

On December 27 the British batteries began bombarding the American ships *Carolina* and *Louisiana*. *Louisiana* fled to safety, but *Carolina* exploded with a roar that rattled windows in New Orleans. On land, the American batteries fired back while Jackson ordered a second line of defense built behind the first. Next day, the British attacked.

At first the Americans in a swamp on the left began to give. But then they steadied, while *Louisiana* poured a plunging fire into the redcoats assaulting the American right. On the ramparts, Lafitte's red-shirted pirates joined the cannonade—and the British assault was broken in blood.

Frustrated in his first attempt, Pakenham now ordered the fleet's big guns brought ashore. On New Year's Eve they were in position behind mounds of earth and hogsheads of sugar about 700 yards away from the American lines. Now, Pakenham thought, his big guns would open a hole in the American ramparts. Then his redcoats would rush through and rout the Americans with the bayonet.

These were basically the tactics which had won for Wellington in his campaigns against Napoleon. Except for improvements in artillery and more widespread use of big guns, warfare had not changed much since the days of the Revolution. The bayonet charge was still the decisive movement. It

39

was the moment of shock and terror which was expected to rout the enemy. Pakenham, therefore, was only following accepted practice when he prepared to pin down the Dirty Shirts with his artillery and then put them to flight with his bayonets.

The Dirty Shirts, meanwhile, were cleaning up. General Jackson had scheduled a full review for New Year's Day. Even though the day dawned raw and foggy, he held to that intention. Visitors from the city streamed into the American camp. Many were ladies in silks. A band played. Troops in clean uniforms carrying burnished steel prepared to parade. Drums beat. But then came a dreadful rolling roar that was neither drums nor thunder, and the mist was slashed with showers of rockets.

Terrified civilians fled for the safety of the city. Soldiers sprinted for the ramparts. Everywhere was confusion, while the British batteries began to take apart Jackson's positions. Cotton bales on the ramparts caught fire. Guns were knocked out. A supply ship was damaged, and when a caisson loaded with ammunition blew up, British soldiers waiting to make the assault set up a confident cheer. That was when the Americans began firing back with their own cannon.

American artillery pierced the hogsheads filled with sugar as though they were empty barrels. American shot crashed among the British guns to smash them and kill their gunners. One by one, Sir Edward's batteries were battered into silence. In the end his big guns were put out of action while the Americans survived practically unscathed.

Sir Edward could hardly believe it, and the most mortified man on the American continent that night was Sir Alexander Cochrane. The contemptible Dirty Shirts had outshot and outfought the conquerors of Napoleon.

Another week passed at New Orleans. Still believing that he could win the war, Sir Edward Pakenham prepared his knockout blow.

On January 8, 1815, some 1,400 men under Colonel William Thornton began to cross the Mississippi in boats. Their mission was to seize the cross-river batteries held by David Morgan's militia and turn them on Jackson's rear. While this happened, three columns would hit Jackson's front. One would be under General Keane along the river on the British left. A second would be in the center under Major General Sir Samuel Gibbs, and the third on the right under Major General John Lambert. The soldiers in this attacking force carried ladders and bundles of sticks called fascines. The fascines were to be thrown into the dry canal to make a crossing, and the ladders were for scaling the ramparts behind the canal.

As the British attack began, Thornton's force got only half its boats into the river. Then, across the river, these vessels were swept downstream below the landing place. Still, Sir Edward

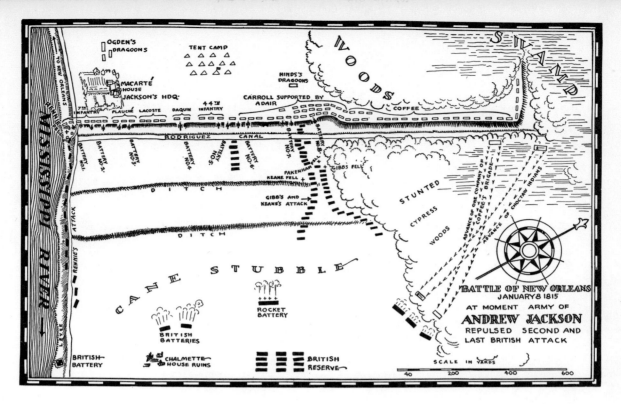

fired his rocket signaling the start of the main attack.

Old Hickory had been up since one o'clock in the morning inspecting his lines. When a foggy daylight came, he was on the left with the force commanded by John Coffee and William Carroll. He was there, standing on a parapet, when Pakenham's rocket burst overhead in a silver-bluish shower. It was answered by another from Keane on the riverbank. Jackson peered intently into the mist. Suddenly, the wind tore a hole in it. Looking through the hole, Old Hickory could see the British advancing.

They came through a stubble of sugar cane. Their crossbelts formed a white X on their scarlet tunics.

"Aim above the cross plates," Jackson ordered.

Then the American cannon roared. The British replied. The fog glowed dull red. It became mixed with smoke. American riflemen could not see through it. Jackson ordered two batteries to cease firing until the air cleared. When it did, cannon to Old Hickory's right opened a heavy fire. The advancing red columns reeled. Steadying, they came on again. Now the Dirty Shirts with their rifles began to take aim.

"Fire!"

Out crashed the volley, coming like a single, shattering crack. Down from the American firing line stepped the first rank of riflemen, making way for the second. Again the order, again the dreadful flash and flame, and the second rank stepped down for the third. For a third time, the mud ramparts breathed fire and smoke, and out among the stubble silvery with frost lay crumpled scarlet coats. General Gibbs's column had been ripped apart. Again and again the American fire

41

A bird's-eye view of the January 8 battlefield near New Orleans, from a sketch by Jackson's

tore into the huddled red fragments, until at last the brave British soldiers were compelled to turn and flee.

"Never before had British veterans quailed," one of Pakenham's officers wrote later. "That leaden torrent no man on earth could face."

Now Sir Edward Pakenham himself came galloping toward his broken right. His horse was shot dead beneath him, and he ran to mount a black pony held for him by an aide. A second

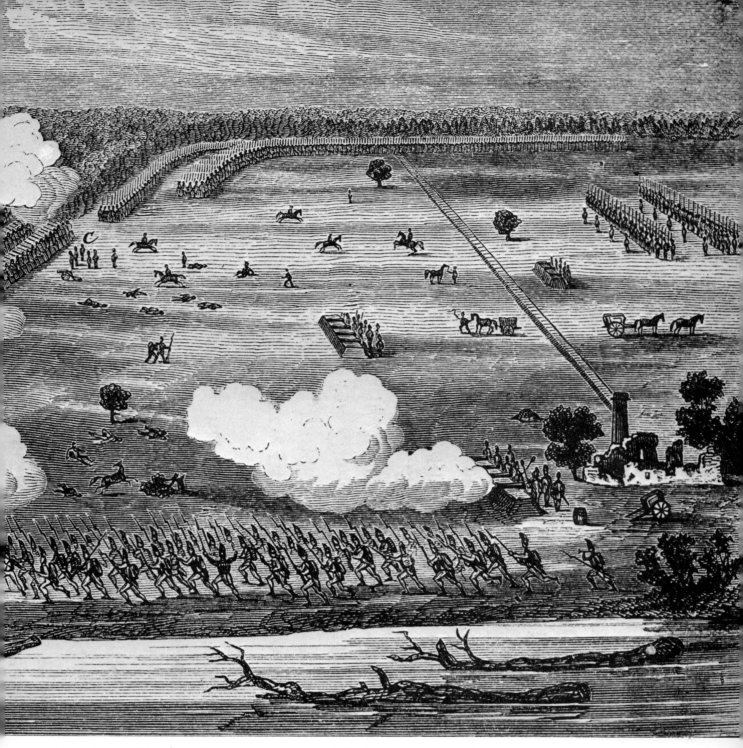

chief engineer. The Americans are entrenched behind the line of fortifications at left.

assault was formed on the right. A "praying regiment" of Highlanders, every man six feet tall or more, went charging through the stubble. But the kilts also fell on that dreadful field. Perhaps 70 Highlanders reached the dry canal, but only 30 reached the top of the rampart—and none of these survived.

Now American marksmanship was cutting down the British leaders. General Gibbs received his death wound.

43

General Jackson exhorting his men to aim above the cross plates of the redcoats' crossbelts.

Keane was down with a ball through the neck, and Pakenham was down and dying. On the British left a brave bayonet charge pierced one American outwork, but that was all. Stunned, General Lambert gave orders to withdraw.

Only across the river did success crown British arms. Here, Colonel Thornton pushed back Morgan's militia. For a while Old Hickory held his breath. If Thornton could bring guns to bear on Jackson's rear, he would be forced to retreat from his fine rampart-and-canal position. But Thornton was recalled by the shaken General Lambert, and the threat passed.

The Battle of New Orleans was over. The British had suffered more than 2,000 casualties, while only seven Americans were killed and six wounded. Looking out toward the bloody cane stubble, an astonished Andrew Jackson saw redcoats arising with upraised hands. He "never had so grand and awful idea of the resurrection," he said, as when he saw "more than 500 Britons emerging from the heaps of their dead comrades, all over the plain rising up, and . . . coming forward . . . as prisoners."

Ten days later, leaving their night fires burning, the British invasion force stole back to their boats. With them went the body of Sir Edward Pakenham encased in a barrel of rum to preserve it.

"What a sight for his wife who is aboard ship," an observer wrote, "and who had hoped to be Governess of Louisiana."

Louisiana, however, would not become British. It would not have changed hands no matter who had won or lost at New Orleans, because the war was already over. Even so, the Battle of New Orleans remains a shining chapter in the annals of American arms. It gave the young nation back its military self-respect. For two years, American forces on land had known little else but defeat and retreat. At New Orleans, Old Glory flew again in victory.

Finally the Battle of New Orleans made a national hero of Andrew Jackson. Chiefly because he had held at New Orleans and given his countrymen back their self-respect, Old Hickory became the seventh President of the United States, and one of the greatest Chief Executives in history.

Another version of the battle, with General Jackson flourishing his hat in the background.

MEXICO CITY
Scott Wins an Empire

Winfield Scott had come to the crossroads of his career. The American general had led his little army about 150 miles from Vera Cruz on the Gulf of Mexico to the city of Puebla, high on the Mexican plateau. Less than a hundred miles away lay Mexico City, the object of Scott's march and the prize sought by President James K. Polk.

Should General Scott pause in Puebla to await reinforcements and badly needed supplies? Or should he cast caution aside and push on? If he waited, General Antonio López de Santa Anna would be granted precious time in which to steady his reeling army and strengthen the defenses of the Mexican capital. Yet, if Scott hurried forward, he would be leading only 10,500 tired troops against a city of 200,000—defended by Santa Anna's army, which Scott believed to be three times the size of his own. He would be cutting himself free of his supply base far to the east in Vera Cruz. In

46

effect, he would be burning his boats behind him, just as the great Hernando Cortez had done 328 years before him.

Winfield Scott was aware of how much his own predicament resembled the plight of the great Spanish conquistador. He was following the very same road that Cortez had taken when he captured the Emperor Montezuma and crushed the Aztecs. Indeed, General Scott had already written to Secretary of War William Marcy: "Like Cortez, finding myself isolated and abandoned, and again like him, always afraid that the next ship or messenger might recall or further cripple me, I resolved no longer to depend on Vera Cruz or home. I would make my little army a self-sustaining machine." He wanted to "throw away the scabbard and advance with the naked blade in hand."

On August 7, 1847, drums beat and bugles blew in Puebla. American doughboys in faded blue formed ranks under the eyes of their officers. Huge and brilliantly uniformed on his splendid horse, Winfield Scott watched his little army go swinging away to Mexico City.

In Britain, when the great Duke of Wellington heard that the American army had cut loose from its base, he said, "Scott is lost. He cannot capture the city, and he cannot fall back on his base."

War with Mexico had come for three reasons: President Polk's desire for California, the unsteadiness of a new Mexican government rocked by revolutions, and the boldness of those American settlers in Mexico who came to be called Texans.

Mexico was one of the last Spanish colonies in the New World to declare her independence of the mother country. In 1824, when Mexico became free, her government had difficulty ruling such a vast territory. It included present-day Mexico as well as the territory that today consists of California, Texas, Nevada, Utah, Arizona, New Mexico and parts of Wyoming and Colorado. Mexico was as big as the United States. Both governments, in order to people their vast uninhabited lands, encouraged immigration. Most of the people moving into Mexico were Americans, who settled in the province of Texas.

Gradually, the Americans came to outnumber the Mexicans in Texas. They dominated the province. Instead of abiding by Mexican laws and customs, they came to live by American standards. In 1836, however, the fiery revolutionary, General Santa Anna, became the virtual dictator of Mexico. He attempted to impose an iron rule upon the Texans. In reply, the Texans declared their independence on March 2, 1836.

Santa Anna retaliated by leading an army north and laying siege to fewer than two hundred Texans gathered in an adobe mission called the Alamo. Although he suffered grievous losses, Santa Anna finally stormed the Alamo, putting all its survivors to death. The

The Mexicans attacking the Alamo.

Mexican chief also shot 350 prisoners taken in another engagement.

Burning for revenge, Texas raised an army under Sam Houston and defeated Santa Anna at the battle of San Jacinto. Now, Texas was truly free, and on March 3, 1837, President Andrew Jackson recognized the Lone Star Republic. Exactly eight years later, Texas was admitted to the Union.

These acts by the American government infuriated the Mexicans. They became even angrier after Texas claimed that its southern boundary

was the Rio Grande, rather than the Nuesces River farther north. Then, when James K. Polk entered the White House and tried to buy California, the Mexicans became so enraged that they broke off relations with the United States. Mexico echoed to calls for war with the arrogant *Yanquis.*

At this point, President Polk ordered General Zachary Taylor to a position "on or near" the Rio Grande to repel invasion. Once again the Mexicans were enraged. For an American army to take a position below the Nuesces

River on territory that the Mexicans believed to be their own was as if a Canadian army had crossed the Niagara River into New York to "defend" Ontario.

Mexico was now torn by civil war in which Santa Anna was ousted. During the fighting, damage estimated at $4.5 million was done to American property. Here, President Polk thought he saw another opportunity. He offered to pay these damage costs if Mexico would recognize the Rio Grande as the southern boundary of Texas. Another $5 million would be paid for New Mexico; and for California "money would be no object." Polk's offers not only were angrily refused, but also caused the downfall of the Mexican government. The new administration began whipping the country into a hate-America frenzy. With this,

Polk ordered General Taylor to move to the north bank of the Rio Grande.

Taylor obeyed. On March 24, 1846, he took up a position opposite the Mexican city of Matamoros. When General Pedro de Ampudia demanded that he withdraw behind the Nuesces River, Taylor refused. Instead, he built a fort and trained his guns on Matamoros. At this point, believing that Taylor was on Mexican soil, the Mexicans attacked him. Eleven Americans were killed.

President Polk then informed Congress that Mexico "has invaded our territory and shed American blood upon the American soil." Blaming Mexico for the outbreak of war, Congress declared that "a state of war exists between that government and the United States." President Polk's tactics of provoking the Mexicans into strik-

General Santa Anna

ing the first blow had been succeesful. On May 13, 1846, he signed the war bill into law.

America had again entered a war unprepared. In 1846, the U.S. Army was down to 5,300 officers and men and was only slightly larger when hostilities commenced. So the nation was compelled to field a force divided between professionals and amateurs.

The professionals were the regular soldiers of the U.S. Army, many of whom were foreigners. Their officers were native-born Americans, tough and trained West Pointers such as Robert E. Lee, Ulysses S. Grant, Albert Sidney Johnston, Joe Johnston, Thomas ("Stonewall") Jackson, George Meade, Pierre Beauregard, George McClellan and many others who later were to oppose each other as the commanding generals of the Civil War.

The amateurs were the "volunteer" regiments raised by the various states and placed under Federal command. This system did away with the militia and the problem of state control. Unfortunately, however, the volunteers were recruited for terms as short as three months and often reached a battlefield just as their enlistments expired and it was time to go home. In addition, the lower officers in the volunteer regiments were elected by the men, and most of the volunteer officers of higher rank were political appointees with little real military experience.

Although some of the American units were equipped with rifles, most of them were armed with muskets, and the Mexican War was fought with weapons and tactics virtually unchanged since Revolutionary days.

The fighting took place at first along the Rio Grande and in the northeastern Mexican department of Nueva Laredo. Here, Zachary Taylor became famous as "Old Rough and Ready," the general who dressed like a doughboy and sometimes rode his horse, Old Whitey, with one leg thrown nonchalantly over the pommel of his saddle. Old Rough and Ready and his regulars defeated the Mexicans at Palo Alto and Resaca de la Palma, captured Matamoros without a fight, stormed Monterrey and defeated Santa Anna at Buena Vista. By then, the Mexican dictator had returned to power, although he also had lost a leg. (Americans who defeated him in a later battle considered his spare wooden leg the finest trophy of the victory.) For Zachary Taylor, the reward for Buena Vista and his other triumphs was national acclaim that would eventually carry him into the White House.

But in February of 1847 it had already been decided that Taylor's theater of operations was not the place to crush Mexico. Instead of hammering uselessly at Mexico's "front door," it would be wiser to slip inside the "side door" at Vera Cruz. Landing here as Cortez had done, an American army could follow Cortez's march to Mexico City and thus duplicate his capture of that capital.

Agreed, but who would command? Polk the politician did not want Taylor, already more popular than he was and obviously hoping for the nomination of the rival Whigs. Unfortunately for Polk, there were no able generals among his own Democrats. At last, he reluctantly selected the Commanding General of the Army, Winfield Scott.

Scott differed from Taylor as much as his nickname of "Old Fuss 'n' Feathers" differed from that of Old Rough and Ready. He was not, however, as fussy as that nickname suggests. He was just precise. This veteran of the War of 1812, who stood six foot four inches tall and was powerfully built, was probably the first truly professional supreme commander in American history. He was so exact in everything he did that when the Americans landed at Vera Cruz they rowed ashore in boats that had been designed to "nest" in sets of three, thus saving space aboard ship.

At Vera Cruz, Scott's blood-and-thunder commanders pleaded with him to storm the city. He refused. That would cost too many lives. Instead, he would take Vera Cruz "by headwork, the slow, scientific progress." So he laid siege to the city and turned the conduct of it over to his engineers. Day after day, Robert E. Lee, Joe Johnston, Pierre Beauregard, George McClellan and the other engineering officers went out to study the city's defenses and to site gun positions. Sometimes U. S. (Sam) Grant of the infantry went along, and once

General Scott's troops land at Vera Cruz to besiege the city, shown in the background at right.

he and Beauregard narrowly escaped death from an exploding enemy shell. At last, Scott's engineers had drawn an investing (siege) line around Vera Cruz. American artillery began bombarding the city. On March 29, 1847, Vera Cruz surrendered. Scott the scientific had triumphed at a loss of only 67 killed and wounded.

It was after this unbloody victory that he began the march that led him to Puebla and the momentous decision to push on to the City of Mexico.

Even Winfield Scott's resourceful engineers felt their hearts sink as they marched down the Cortez road into the splendid Valley of Mexico and saw the defenses of Mexico City. General Santa Anna had skillfully fortified the network of lakes and marshes screening his capital. Passage between the lakes was possible only on causeways raised above them. These were heavily guarded by Santa Anna's army of 25,000 men.

Winfield Scott saw clearly that he could not storm the enemy's outer fortifications without suffering frightful losses. He sent his engineers out to reconnoiter. They found a rough but passable road, by which the army moved to the village of San Agustín (modern Tlalpan) nine miles south of the city.

Yet here, too, the Americans seemed stopped. A few miles ahead of them was the fortified hacienda of San Antonio. Two miles farther north lay the Río Churubusco, covered by forts and a fortified bridge. Ahead of Scott, the route was barred. To his right or east, he was stymied by Lake Xochimilco. On his left or west was the Pedregal, a field of gray lava looking like a sea of frozen stone. The Pedregal also looked impassable.

But then on August 18 Captain Robert E. Lee led a party of engineers into the Pedregal. He found a tiny track through it. Following it, Lee came to a pile of volcanic rock. He climbed it and saw the San Angel road in front of him, and to his left Mexican troops on a slope in the village of Padierna.

Captain Lee reported to General Scott that he believed the Pedregal track could be widened to allow guns and wagons to move over it. Work was begun and an American force under General Gideon Pillow did move over it. Then General Pillow ordered two of his brigades across the San Angel road to cut off the Mexicans at Padierna from their main base in Mexico City. That night, the brigade commanders decided to move around to the rear of the Mexicans and surprise them. As they did, a storm broke —drenching Captain Lee as he moved over the rain-swept Pedregal to lead still another American brigade across the road and into the Mexican rear.

Early in the morning of August 20, 1847, the Americans in front of Padierna began firing. The Mexicans fired back. Then, to their astonishment and terror, they heard other *Yanquis* yelling fiercely in their rear. A tide of

52

BATTLE GROUNDS
around
MEXICO
Taken by permission from
Humboldt's Valley of Mexico

blue came flowing down the slope behind them. Frantic, some of the Mexican gunners tried to reverse their guns and fire. But it was too late. The blue tide burst upon them and the Mexicans broke and ran. In 17 minutes the battle was over. The brightening light of dawn shone on the San Angel road, black with Santa Anna's soldiers in full retreat.

Now General Scott was free to come up on San Antonio in its rear.

Santa Anna saw his peril and abandoned the hacienda at San Antonio. Pulling back two miles, he occupied the northern side of the Río Churubusco. Here his soldiers moved into the *garita* or gates which guarded the heads of causeways. Actually, the gates were fortified stone buildings used as police and customs stations. Linked to them was the fortified convent of San Mateo and the fortified bridge. Into this complex the Americans came crashing "butt-end first."

Five American brigades made the attack, engaging Santa Anna all across his front and also trying to turn his right flank across the Churubusco. The Mexicans fought back with bravery and skill. For three hours they held the Americans in check. They pinned down one brigade in a cornfield beside the San Antonio road. Their bullets came so thick that the sound of them hitting stalks was like the sound of popping corn. It seemed that Winfield

Americans storm a bridgehead during the Battle of Churubusco.

Scott had been defeated. He had all of his available men in action—6,000 against about 18,000. They were falling by the score, and one officer near Scott thought: We must succeed or the army is lost.

Undaunted, the Americans pressed forward. Fortunately for them, the Mexicans had begun to run low on ammunition. Almost at once the American lines heaved forward on three fronts. Their advance was irresistible. Only the San Mateo convent still stood fast. Here a battalion of deserters from the American army fought desperately, like "men with halters around their necks." They held out until there were only 80 of them left. These were finally overpowered and taken prisoner—many of them to be hung later for desertion.

And so General Santa Anna ordered another withdrawal north.

Winfield Scott might have pursued him all the way into Mexico City, and perhaps ended the war right then and there. But Scott had suffered 1,000 casualties. His losses were far less than Santa Anna's casualties of about 4,000 killed and wounded, and 3,200 soldiers captured. But Scott believed his enemy was defeated, and he granted an armistice during which a peace was to be negotiated.

Santa Anna, however, wanted the truce as a breathing spell in which to strengthen his forces. When Winfield Scott realized that he had been deceived, he ordered the armistice ended and began attacking again.

The first objective of the renewed American assault was the Molino del Rey, or "King's Mill." It was a massive stone building standing west of mighty Chapultepec Castle, which guarded the western approaches to Mexico City. Scott wanted to capture it because it would crack Santa Anna's line. The American general had also heard that the Molino was being used as a foundry to cast new cannon from church bells. His choice as commander for the operation was General William Worth, a hell-for-leather commander who unfortunately believed that bayonets could breach stone walls.

On September 8, 1847, Worth sent about 3,250 soldiers charging forward with only the barest of artillery preparation.

Unscathed, the Mexicans in the Molino struck at the Americans with a blaze of musketry and cannon shot. The blue lines were bowled over. Still the *Yanquis* charged. Again they took terrible casualties, but eventually they battered in one of the Molino's gates and went rushing into its murky interior. Now, the stubborn Mexicans were forced to yield the Molino and fall back on Chapultepec.

Nevertheless, Worth's force had suffered grievously. Even though Santa Anna lost 680 prisoners and between 1,000 and 2,000 killed and wounded, Worth had lost close to 800 men—almost a quarter of his command. One of Scott's officers confided to his diary that night: "We were like Pyrrhus after

55

The Battle of Molino del Rey. The mill (center background) protects

the fight with Fabricius—a few more such 'victories' and this army would be destroyed."

Whittled away as his forces were, General Winfield Scott *had* to attack again. He was down to 7,000 battle-weary men. His army was at the end

of a 250-mile supply line. His base at Vera Cruz, from which his supplies were forwarded, was then in the grip of yellow fever. Scott had to crush Santa Anna before the Mexican war chief realized that he could get behind Scott, cut his supply line and isolate him. Therefore, the question at his

56

Chapultepec Castle on the hill at right.

war council the day after the Molino battle was not *when* to attack but *where*.

Captain Lee and the volunteer generals favored the southern approach, but Lieutenant Beauregard and the regular generals preferred Chapultepec in the west. After Beauregard

pointed out that the fall of Chapultepec would leave the causeways into the city open, General Franklin Pierce (who would live to become fourteenth President of the United States) changed his vote to Chapultepec.

"Gentlemen," said Scott, "we shall attack by the western gates."

Dawn of September 13, 1847, broke with the roar of American artillery battering Chapultepec's walls. Then an American force made a feint south of Mexico City to deceive Santa Anna. It worked. When General Nicolas Bravo in Chapultepec called for reinforcements, Santa Anna refused his appeal. He had his eyes fixed to the south. So Bravo had to hang on with less than 1,000 men, of whom 100 were young cadets quartered at the Military College in Chapultepec.

Against them came General Pillow's division from the west and General John Quitman's division from the southeast. On the west Pillow's men were fragmented by a withering Mexican fire. Pillow was wounded and his men pinned down in a ditch under the castle wall. There they found that no one had brought the ladders required to scale the walls. Desperate, Pillow called for help. Finally the ladders arrived and were propped up against the wall. The Americans went swarming up them. Lieutenant James Longstreet came rushing up with the American flag, and was shot down. But Lieutenant George Pickett caught the falling colors and carried them over the wall.

57

General Winfield Scott (seated) in later years.

On Pillow's left, Lieutenant Tom Jackson was trying to get one of his guns into action. But his men broke under enemy fire. Standing alone among dead gunners and kicking horses, the lanky, awkward young officer—who was not yet called "Stonewall"—cried out, "There's no danger! See, I'm not hit!" But his men could hear the whistling musket balls, and they refused to come forward until more artillery appeared.

Farther east, General Quitman's division was being riddled. Americans and Mexicans fought hand to hand with clubbed muskets and swinging, clanging swords. Then the Mexicans fell back through the gate. Yelling, the Americans pursued. They broke the enemy—all, that is, but the gallant

58

cadets of the Military College. By their stand they became immortal in Mexican history as *Los Niños,* or "The Young Ones." Six of them aged 13 to 19 were killed. One of these, 18-year-old Agustín Melgar, dueled the Americans step by step up the staircase until he was at last caught and bayoneted on the roof. It was then that the green-red-and-white Mexican tricolor was pulled down, and the red-white-and-blue hauled up in its place.

Now, with Chapultepec fallen, the battle became a race between General Quitman and General Worth for Mexico City. Quitman had the closer route, moving along a causeway running directly to the Belén Gate. Worth had to follow another causeway north before swinging east to advance on the San Cosmé Gate. Quitman won. At 1:20 in the afternoon, his troops punched through the Belén Gate into the city's outskirts. Suddenly, bugles blew and Mexicans led by Santa Anna himself sallied from the Citadel and from Belén Prison. Quitman's soldiers and Marines halted them, and then hung on desperately.

General Worth's division also took heavy casualties while driving on San Cosmé. Hearing that this entrance into the city might fall, Santa Anna hurried there. But his presence made little difference. Keeping clear of the streets down which the Mexicans were firing, Worth's men seized picks and crowbars and began burrowing a path through the walls of the houses. By nightfall they were inside the city—

and by then Santa Anna decided to abandon his capital and flee.

On the morning of September 14, 1847, General John Quitman led his troops forward. He was an odd sight, his left foot being bare from the loss of his shoe the day before. Just as his units moved out, the Mexicans sent forward a flag of truce. Quitman took possession of the Citadel. Then, hearing that convicts freed by the fleeing Santa Anna were plundering the city, he put himself at the head of his men and marched into the Grand Plaza. Forming on the great square in the shadow of the Cathedral, he ordered his Marines to clear the National Palace of vagabonds and looters.

The Palace contained the legendary "Halls of Montezuma," and on its roof that day Lieutenant A. S. Nicholson cut down the Mexican flag and ran up Old Glory. Thus, he gave to his Marine Corps the first few words of its famous song. Below him, Quitman and his troops stiffened. There was a clatter of horses' hoofs. General Winfield Scott, huge and commanding on a superb horse, swept into the Plaza, escorted by dragoons with bared sabers.

Mexico City had fallen, and even the Mexican civilians peering cautiously from their windows above the Plaza cheered and waved their handkerchiefs at the conquering General Scott. Soon afterward the detested Santa Anna fell from power. On February 2, 1848, the Treaty of Guada-

General Scott triumphantly enters the Grand Plaza of Mexico City.

lupe Hidalgo was signed, ending the war.

It was largely because of this treaty that the United States became what it is today: a huge continental power stretching from the Atlantic all the way to the Pacific. Mexico ceded to the United States an area more than five times the size of France. True enough, this huge territorial expansion was achieved by a war of doubtful moral justification. True also, the Mexican War is probably the most outstanding example of American interference in Latin American affairs, an arrogant attitude which was not to be reversed until 1933, when Franklin Roosevelt announced his "Good Neighbor" policy.

Yet, if there is blame for the Mexican War, it belongs to James K. Polk —not Winfield Scott. To Scott belongs the glory of winning the most profitable war in American history. He had risked all to gain all. He had made Hernando Cortez his model, and in the end he had surpassed the great conquistador himself.

CHANCELLORSVILLE
The Tragic Triumph
of Lee and Jackson

The fruits of the Mexican victory were sour with the seeds of discord over slavery. The South wanted the vast new territories opened to its "peculiar institution" of slave labor. The North did not.

North and South seethed with dispute and debate over bondage. Finally, the Compromise of 1850 was reached. On the one hand California was to be admitted as a free rather than a slave state. On the other hand the North was to obey a new and strict Fugitive Slave Law.

Unfortunately, the Compromise satisfied no one. Northerners openly refused to return fugitive slaves to their owners. The group called the Abolitionists demanded outright abolition of slavery. Harriet Beecher Stowe published her famous book, *Uncle Tom's Cabin,* which attacked slavery as a moral evil. Now the South was enraged. Angry Southern leaders talked of seceding from the Union. They defended slavery as morally just and said that the North was trying to eliminate it just to weaken the South.

Then a Northerner named John Brown attacked and seized the Federal arsenal at Harpers Ferry. His purpose was to arm the Negro slaves for an uprising in the South.

John Brown was captured by a company of Marines under Colonel Robert E. Lee. Brown was tried and convicted of murder and treason and on December 2, 1859, he was hung.

In John Brown, the Abolitionists found a martyr. They called him a "new saint" and said he had been sacrificed on the altar of slavery. To the South, John Brown had been the embodiment of all their fears.

"He wanted to arm the slaves!" Southerners cried. "That's what the North *really* wants."

Although the cooler heads and moderates of both sides pleaded for reason and restraint, the people of both regions began to hate each other with a blind, irrational passion. Then in May, 1860, the new anti-slavery Republican Party nominated a tall, lanky, prairie lawyer named Abraham Lincoln for President. Some of the more enraged Southern states announced that if Lincoln was elected in November they would secede from the Union.

Abraham Lincoln was elected, and on December 20, 1860, South Carolina did secede. She was followed out of the Union by Mississippi, Alabama, Georgia, Florida, Louisiana and Texas. On February 8, 1861, the seven seceded states met in Montgomery, Alabama. They formed the Confederate States of America and elected Jefferson Davis its first president. They were later joined by Virginia, North Carolina, Arkansas and Tennessee.

Because a President in those days did not take office until the March following his election, four months passed before Lincoln was inaugurated. During that interval, the South made itself strong and the Southern firebrands gained the upper hand over the moderates. Hoping to force powerful Virginia to join the Confederacy, the firebrands moved to capture the Federal bastion at Fort Sumter off the South Carolina coast. But Sumter refused to surrender. At 4:30 in the morning of April 12, 1861, a Confederate mortar on the Charleston shore fired on the fort—and with that shot the Civil War began.

The American Civil War was the first mass war of the era of modern warfare. This was because modern arms had undergone two revolutions: the Democratic and the Industrial.

The Democratic Revolution first affected warfare during the French Revolution, when the *levée en masse* made every man, woman and child in the nation obliged to serve the national war effort. Every able-bodied Frenchman was also liable to service in the army. Other nations quickly adopted

The Confederates fire on Fort Sumter.

this practice of "conscripting" or drafting men. That is, instead of being asked to fight for pay or for patriotism, men were *made* to serve. This happened in the Civil War, when both the Confederate and the Federal governments drafted huge armies.

The Industrial Revolution, with its telegraph and railroads and mass manufacturing techniques, made it possible to move these large armies rapidly and to keep them supplied and armed.

The Industrial Revolution also gave them improved weapons with which to slaughter each other. Thus, men went to battle faster, with better weapons and in greater numbers. The result: carnage.

Out of the Industrial Revolution there also came the mass-produced rifle which was to work such a radical change in warfare. For two centuries the musket and the bayonet had dominated battle. But the killing range of

63

the smooth-bore musket was no more than 100 yards. Because it was inaccurate and took time to load, the musket had usually been used only for the single volley which preceded the bayonet charge. The Battle of New Orleans, of course, had shown what happened to bayonet charges launched against entrenched marksmen. But no one paid heed.

Now came the grooved-bore rifle with a much longer range than the smooth-bore musket. However, it was hard to make a bullet for the muzzle-loading rifle. It had to be small enough to be dropped down the bore and rammed home—yet large enough to grip the grooves in the rifle bore. This problem was solved by the Minié ball, named for the French inventor of that name. When fired, the Minié ball expanded, gripping the rifle grooves and thus making use of the powerful powder gases exploding behind it. With the Minié ball, the killing range rose from 100 to 500 yards. The defense, of course, became even more formidable, a dreadful fact which none of the Civil War generals realized. This, then, helps to explain the frightful losses which occurred when the Civil War exploded in all its fury.

Most of the fighting took place in two main areas: the Western Theater, a region generally west of the Cumberland Mountains, and the Eastern Theater, mostly in northern Virginia. In the West, Federal fortunes rose gradually and in proportion to the growing skill of General Ulysses S. Grant. In the East, the Union cause suffered grievously, chiefly because of the fighting prowess of the Rebel soldiers of the Army of Northern Virginia and the military mastery of General Lee.

Robert Edward Lee was the flower of Southern chivalry. Winfield Scott always called him the "hero" of the Mexican War, and his brother officers described him as the handsomest man in the Army. In June, 1861, when Lee took command of the Army of Northern Virginia, he was 54 years old and looked like a very god of war. Whenever this tall, gray-bearded soldier rode among his men on his great gray stallion Traveler, his soldiers stood in awe and took off their slouch hats as though their beloved "Marse Robert" were truly more than human.

"I've heard of God," a Confederate lady exclaimed, "but I've *seen* General Lee."

Jove of war that he was, Lee was also very gentle. Once, when a wounded Union soldier cried out to him defiantly, he took the youth's hand, looked lovingly into his eyes and said, "My son, I hope you will soon be well."

Lee the engineer was a master of defensive warfare. His men called him the "King of Spades" because he always had them digging entrenchments. Lee was also a daring offensive fighter. Again and again, his bold gambles in the face of superior numbers defeated the North's Army of the Potomac and forced it to retreat. Never, it seemed,

64

was Marse Robert at a loss for a maneuver that would turn the tide. Rarely did he entrust execution of it to anyone but General Thomas "Stonewall" Jackson.

General Jackson gained his nickname during the First Battle of Bull Run, when a Confederate general cried, "There is Jackson standing like a stone wall!"

True enough, Jackson's brigade did hold like a wall. But the nickname was hardly appropriate for a swift, tigerish commander such as Jackson. He might better have been compared to a panther than to a wall.

At first glance, however, Jackson seemed like neither. Forever sucking a lemon, he was a silent, awkward figure aboard his shambling horse Little Sorrel. His big feet were turned out in the stirrups and his uniforms hung on him loosely. Only the lemon and his brown beard were visible beneath his shabby forage cap. The cap's broken visor was always pulled down, concealing his pale blue eyes.

Stonewall Jackson was like a warrior out of the Old Testament. In action, his eyes gleamed with a holy fire. He was always quoting the Bible, and whenever he triumphed he gave all the credit to God. If he was denied a victory, he blamed the setback on his own sins. In his low voice, Jackson would call an officer a "wicked fellow" for swearing. Yet, in the same soft murmur he told an officer regretful at having killed brave Federals, "No, shoot them all. I do not wish them to be brave."

Such a general, swift, fearless and

The opponents at Chancellorsville: General Stonewall Jackson (left) and General Joseph Hooker.

relentless, was just the man to execute Lee's daring maneuvers. Again and again, Lee and Jackson discomfited the overconfident Federals. General after general went down before them. After four Union generals—McDowell, McClellan, Pope and Burnside—had failed to capture the Confederate capital at Richmond, a dismayed President Lincoln named General Joseph Hooker commander of the Army of the Potomac.

Like General Lee, "Fighting Joe" Hooker was a handsome soldier. Broad-shouldered and fair, with a complexion "as delicate and silken as a woman's," he was a clean-shaven exception to the Civil War rule of flowing beards and curling mustaches. He was also profane and a hard drinker, although he swore off drink once he took command of the Army of the Potomac. Thereafter, his driving energy and blistering tongue whipped his command into a much-improved fighting force. In all, Fighting Joe had 94,000 superbly equipped and well-trained troops when, in April of 1863, he moved against Richmond.

Opposing him was General Lee, with about 53,000 men. The Army of Northern Virginia was concentrated along the Rappahannock River near Fredericksburg. As usual, it was well entrenched. Realizing the folly of attacking the King of Spade's fixed position, Hooker devised a plan to lure Lee out of his fortifications. He sent General John Sedgwick and 40,000

men down to Fredericksburg. Sedgwick was to "demonstrate" down there —that is, by his mere presence to hold Lee in position. Meanwhile, Hooker took 54,000 men up the Rappahannock to cross the river and come down on Lee's left flank.

Moving with speed and skill, Hooker had most of his troops over the river and advancing on Lee's open flank before Marse Robert realized what was happening. On April 29, Hooker came to Chancellorsville, a place which gained its name from Mr. Chancellor's little brick house in a crossroads clearing. Chancellorsville was in "the Wilderness," a murky tangle of tall trees and thick bushes laced with narrow streams and swamps. Visibility in the Wilderness was poor, and it was difficult for large bodies of troops to pass through it. It delayed the Union Army's progress. Meanwhile Robert E. Lee saw through Sedgwick's demonstration at Fredericksburg. Realizing that his left was in danger, he ordered Jubal Early and 10,000 men to hold off Sedgwick, while Lee hurried upriver to confront Hooker.

Even so, Hooker had a golden opportunity. On his own front he had Lee outflanked and outnumbered. Down at Fredericksburg, Sedgwick could easily crash through Early and smash into Lee's rear. In other words, Hooker had the great Confederate general caught between two fires.

Fighting Joe, however, did not see it that way. Suddenly turning cautious, he let Sedgwick sit still and ordered his own force to fall back on Chancellorsville. It was an astounding turnabout, and the reason for it seems to be that Hooker had lost confidence in himself. He did not admit that even to himself, informing his officers that the idea now was to fall back on a strong position and dig in. Then, when Lee attacked, the Rebels would be destroyed. Some of Hooker's commanders were dismayed by this decision. They realized that their general was handing over the initiative to Lee. They knew also that Robert Edward Lee was no man to do what his opponent expected him to do.

That night, May 1, Lee and Stonewall Jackson made plans to strike Hooker. They met on a road about a mile southeast of Chancellorsville. But as they stood there talking a Federal sharpshooter began sniping at them, and they moved off the road into a clump of pine trees. There they sat down, side by side. As always, General Lee was impeccable and imposing in his handsome gray tunic. Stonewall, however, looked decidedly different. He no longer wore his familiar faded

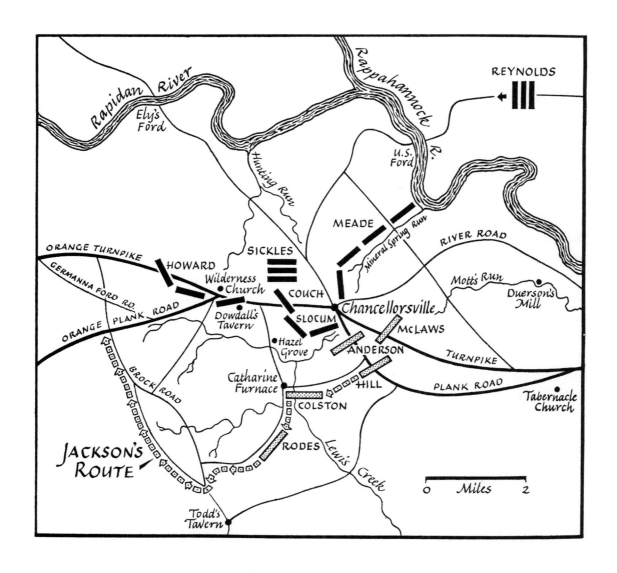

Generals Lee (left) and Jackson on the night of May 1, planning their attack at Chancellorsville.

uniform but rather the bright new gold-braided one given him by his friend, Jeb Stuart. But he was the same closed-mouthed Jackson, more silent than ever now that he was in the presence of the one man on earth he would follow blindly.

At first, Lee and Jackson agreed that they should examine the enemy's center, the very spot which Hooker hoped that they would hit. Engineers were ordered to probe the Union middle. But then Jeb Stuart rode up, huge and merry as ever, bursting with the news that Hooker's right flank was "in the air." That meant that it was open to attack. Lee's eyes gleamed and so did Jackson's. Here was their chance.

When the engineers came back to report that the Union center was too strong to be attacked, the generals hardly heeded them.

"How can we get at these people?" Lee mused, searching the map resting on his knees.

"You know best." Stonewall replied. "Show me what to do, and we will do it."

Lee put a finger on the map. He traced a line westward toward Hooker's open right flank. That would be it, he said. Stonewall's pale eyes gleamed again. He arose with one of his rare smiles, saluted and said, "My troops will move at four o'clock."

After a few more words, the two

men parted—each to sleep on blankets spread upon the pine needles, a saddle for a pillow.

Awaking shortly before four in the morning, Jackson sent staff officers to scout his line of march. They returned after Lee rejoined him, and both men were overjoyed to learn that there was a good road leading to Hooker's right. It ran through the woods, and Jackson's troops and guns could move along it without being seen.

"General Jackson," Lee asked, "what do you propose to do?"

Stonewall pointed to the route shown him by his officers, and said, "Go around here."

"What do you propose to make this movement with?"

"With my whole corps," Jackson replied.

Lee was momentarily silent before asking, "What will you leave me?"

When Stonewall indicated that he was taking nearly 30,000 men with him, leaving his chief with a bare 14,000 opposite Hooker's mighty host, Lee fell silent again. It would be a terrible risk. If Hooker changed his mind again and decided to resume the attack while Jackson was away, he would have the weakened Lee at his mercy. But Lee the gambler was used to taking such risks. He did not flinch from the odds.

In an instant Lee had murmured, "Well, go on," and the great dare at Chancellorsville was begun.

Fighting Joe Hooker was also up early that morning. His confidence had returned, and he had already told his officers, "The enemy is in my power, and God Almighty cannot deprive me of them."

Inspecting his lines that morning of May 2, Hooker kept murmuring, "How strong! How strong!" When he received a report that his outposts had sighted a large Rebel column moving west toward his right, he was delighted. Lee was retreating! Bobby Lee had backed off from Fighting Joe Hooker! Jubilant as he was, Hooker was still wary. Lee might be up to something. So he sent a message to the one-armed General O. O. Howard holding down his right: "We have good reason to suppose that the enemy is moving to our right."

Back came the confident reply: "I am taking measures to resist an attack from the west."

Those "measures," however, amounted to no more than two hub-to-hub guns facing west supported by two regiments totaling about 900 men. This light force was all that held Howard's extreme right flank. Otherwise, it was truly "in the air." Like Hooker, Howard was overconfident. He believed that the Rebels were making a show of force designed to conceal a retreat.

So Howard's men lounged and talked or played cards on that bright May afternoon. As the sun sank lower in the sky, it seemed less and less likely that the enemy would attack. Dinner call came, and the soldiers in blue—

most of them Germans from New York and Pennsylvania—casually stacked their arms to eat. Suddenly, groups of deer came bounding out of the woods to their right. Frightened rabbits came hopping after them. The Union soldiers laughed and cheered. They did not wonder who or what had alarmed the animals. Carefree in the setting sun reddening the western treetops like fire, they merely whooped and cheered.

The road westward was just wet enough to be cool to the tread and free from dust. For this, the marching Rebels were thankful. They were also grateful for a golden spring day, which might be the last for many of them. The woods were bright with new green leaves. White and pink dogwood blossoms brushed their shoulders as they marched. Sometimes they looked up when they heard General Jackson's familiar voice urging them on: "Press forward! Press forward!"

Stonewall was anxious. His start had been delayed for hours, and if he did not hurry he would not have much daylight left in which to attack. Then, at two o'clock in the afternoon, he was met by Fitzhugh Lee, the burly nephew of the commanding general. Lee drew rein beside Jackson on Little Sorrel.

"General," he said, "if you will ride with me, I will show you the enemy's right."

Accompanied by a courier, the two men rode off. They came to a little hill, which they climbed on horseback.

On its summit Jackson drew back a branch thick with leaves. There below, and only a few hundred yards away, was the Union right. There the Federal soldiers stood in groups, laughing, talking, smoking. To their rear other soldiers were butchering cattle. Soon, as the trembling Jackson guessed, the enemy would be sitting down to dine.

Galloping back to his troops, Stonewall Jackson ordered them to get into line across the Union right. They were to shape a T, making themselves the crossbar perpendicular to the shaft formed by the Union line. It took a long time for so many men to form a two-mile line. As brigade after brigade of men in butternut and gray marched into position, Jackson watched them in an agony of suspense. He glanced again and again at his watch. At 5:15 he could wait no longer, even though his lines were only two-thirds formed. There was only an hour and a half of daylight left.

Looking up from the watch in his hand, Stonewall spoke quietly to General Robert Rodes beside him. "Are you ready, General Rodes?"

"Yes, sir."

"You can go forward, then."

Into the screen of brush and stunted trees surged the Confederates. Brambles tore at their clothes. Halfway to the Federal line, the Rebels were in tatters. Now they were flushing deer. Soon the cottontails of frightened rabbits were bobbing through the woods.

Those were the fleeing animals that so amused General Howard's carefree

Confederate soldiers overrunning General Howard's position.

soldiers. But then there came a ripple of rifle shots, and the laughter died in the Federals' throats. Now they heard the high weird yipping of the Rebel yell, thick rolling volleys of musketry, the boom of cannon. Out of the sun-red forest, screaming and sprinting forward, came Jackson's leading troops.

They burst upon the terrified Federals in irresistible waves. The two Union regiments facing west were brushed aside like straw, and their two abandoned guns seized and turned upon their comrades. Within minutes the turnpike to the Union rear was thronged with fleeing Federals.

General Howard rode forward to check the rout. An abandoned flag clamped under his stump of an arm, fighting to control his skittish horse with his good arm, the bareheaded general pleaded with his soldiers to halt and re-form. Tears rolled down his cheeks as he called to them. But they ignored him, flowing around him in a frightened flood. Some of them cut their packs from their backs as they ran, so eager were they to escape the Confederate wrath.

After them came Jackson's yelling soldiers. Stonewall was among them, riding Little Sorrel.

"Push right ahead," he called,

General Jackson urging on his long line of troops.

72

swinging his arm like a man battering down a wall.

Suddenly, there came the muted sound of cannon to the east. Jackson's eyes gleamed. Lee was attacking! He was keeping Hooker off balance, while Jackson rolled up the Union right flank.

Now that flank was utterly gone, and Stonewall Jackson was in a frenzy of suppressed excitement. He wanted to get in behind Hooker and cut off his retreat across the Rappahannock. But his men were tiring and darkness was falling. Still, Jackson had four fresh brigades left. They were commanded by General A. P. Hill. Stonewall ordered them in.

"Press them!" cried Jackson. "Cut them off from the river, Hill! Press them!"

But it was not possible to press the pursuit immediately. The darkness made movement difficult, and General Hill needed time to get his troops into position. Moreover, the Federals had at last rallied. Hooker was rushing troops to his right, and his artillery was striking savagely at the exhausted Rebels. Soon exploding shells had set parts of the Wilderness on fire. Smoke and flames rose above the battlefield, and the rising full moon glowed red. But then the moon brightened, turning gold as it soared above the smoke. In its light, Stonewall Jackson rode forward to reconnoiter. He was determined to send General Hill's force out on a moonlit pursuit.

Satisfied that the Federals were not in position to resist him, Stonewall drew rein and turned to ride back the way he had come. With him were staff officers. In all, there were nearly twenty horsemen in Stonewall's party. As they approached their own pickets, the Rebel soldiers mistook them for Union cavalry. The Confederate pickets opened fire, and three of their shots struck General Jackson. Two pierced his left arm and the third passed through his hand.

Shocked and bleeding, he was lifted from his horse. While the frantic Little Sorrel scampered off for the Federal lines, Jackson was taken in an ambulance to an emergency hospital at Wilderness Tavern. There his left arm was amputated. Command passed to A. P. Hill, and after Hill was wounded Jeb Stuart took over. Even though Stuart renewed the attack, most of the momentum passed from Jackson's great flanking stroke.

The shaken Hooker had begun falling back. Stunned by a falling pillar in Mr. Chancellor's house, he temporarily relinquished command of the Army of the Potomac. Then, regaining both his composure and his command, Hooker ordered Sedgwick to attack the Rebels at Fredericksburg.

With this, the masterful Robert E. Lee calmly turned his back on Hooker and marched east to hurl Sedgwick back across the river. Facing west again, he marched back to Chancellorsville to strike at Hooker. But by then Fighting Joe Hooker had had enough of Marse Robert. One by one, he got his crestfallen divisions across the Rappahannock. Soon President Lincoln and the entire North were dismayed to learn that the fifth attempt to conquer Richmond had met with greater disaster than the previous four.

Although Chancellorsville was to rank as Robert E. Lee's greatest victory, it brought little but disappointment to the Confederate commander. His objective had been to crush Hooker or else to compel him to surrender his army, and in this he had been thwarted. Moreover, even as the Union Army crept away in defeat, Lee was gravely concerned for the great lieutenant who had made his greatest victory possible.

At first, Stonewall Jackson seemed to be making a good recovery from the amputation of his arm. But then he came down with pneumonia. Hearing this, the grieving Lee told Jackson's chaplain, "Give him my affectionate regards, and tell him to make haste and get well, and come back to me as soon

The Federal retreat at Chancellorsville.

as he can. He has lost his left arm, but I have lost my right."

Soon the stricken Stonewall was drifting in and out of consciousness. The entire South held its breath. Newspapers insisted that General Jackson could not die. God would not deprive the South's cause of such a leader, they reasoned. Yet Stonewall worsened. His wife was by his side, and she burst into tears when the doctor informed her that her husband could not live.

"Oh, no," Jackson murmured. "You are frightened. Death is not so near. I may yet get well."

Sobbing, Anna Jackson burst out that the doctor had said there was no hope.

Seeming surprised, Jackson called for his physician. "Doctor," he said, "Anna informs me that you have told her I am to die today. Is it so?"

The doctor said it was.

Jackson pondered a moment. "Very good, very good," he said, using a favorite phrase. "It is all right." He fell silent for a moment. Then he said, "It is the Lord's day. My wish is fulfilled. I have always desired to die on Sunday."

Early in the afternoon of May 10, 1863, Stonewall Jackson drifted into delirium. He prayed and gave commands by turns. A few minutes before three o'clock, he called out, "Order A. P. Hill to prepare for action! Pass the infantry to the front . . . Tell Major Hawks—" Jackson did not finish the sentence.

But then, smiling, speaking as though relieved, as though a crisis had passed or a battle had been won, he spoke his last words.

"Let us cross over the river," he said, "and rest under the shade of the trees."

APPOMATTOX
Grant and Sheridan
End the War

Shortly after the Civil War began, the Confederate General Richard Ewell told a friend, "There is one West Pointer, I think in Missouri, little known, and whom I hope the Northern people will not find out. I mean Sam Grant. I knew him well at the Academy and in Mexico. I should fear him more than any of their officers I have yet heard of. He is not a man of genius, but he is clear-headed, quick and daring."

The North almost did not "find out" about Ulysses Simpson Grant. After the Mexican War, he became bored by the tedium of the peacetime Army and began to drink so heavily that he was forced to resign his commission rather than face a court-martial. Thereafter he passed through a series of failures: as a farmer on "Hardscrabble Farm" in Missouri, as a real-estate salesman, as a down-and-outer selling firewood in St. Louis and finally as an ordinary clerk in his family's harness shop in Galena, Illinois.

Everyday life apparently bored Grant. But he flourished on adversity, always rising to a crisis. Once, when an armed customer stormed into the family store, it was Grant who calmly took the gun away from him. When wild horses needed to be gentled, it was again he who was called upon. Grant, one of the finest horsemen to come out of West Point, had a way with beasts as well as men. There was something in his voice that attracted and calmed the animals he loved so well, while the men who served under him remarked upon the clarity of his commands.

After the outbreak of the Civil War, Grant received a new commission as a colonel of volunteers. His first victory was a bloodless one over a Colonel Harris in Missouri. Approaching the Rebel camp, Grant felt afraid. But he pressed on and found to his amazement that Harris had fled. "It occurred to me at once," Grant wrote later, "that Harris had been as much afraid of me as I had been of him. This was a view of the question I had never taken before; but it was one I never forgot afterward."

Thereafter, Grant led Union troops to triumph after triumph. After he demanded and received the unconditional surrender of Fort Donelson in Tennessee—and because the phrase fitted his initials—he became famous as "Unconditional Surrender" Grant. His greatest victory, however, was at

President Lincoln (left) gives Ulysses S. Grant his commission as lieutenant general in charge of all Northern armies.

Vicksburg. Capture of this Rebel stronghold on the Mississippi River cut the Confederacy in two and turned the Big Muddy into a Union canal. Next, General Grant lifted the Rebel siege at Chattanooga. It was there that a cocky little spitfire of a general named Phil Sheridan came to Grant's attention.

Standing only five feet five inches, weighing less than 130 pounds, black-haired Phil Sheridan was all drive and daring. He fought at the head of his troops, never behind them. Because he was such a fighter, Grant took Sheridan east when Abraham Lincoln called Grant to Washington and put him in command of all the Union armies.

When Grant took command on March 9, 1864, the Confederacy was on the defensive. Grant's own victories in the Western Theater had forced the South back on its own territory, and in the East the Battle of Gettysburg had repulsed Robert E. Lee's invasion of the North.

General Grant saw clearly that the time had come for an all-out drive in both theaters. In the Western Theater, he ordered William Tecumseh Sherman to advance from Tennessee into Georgia. In the Eastern Theater, he ordered the Army of the Potomac to advance on Lee in Virginia. Grant accompanied the Army of the Potomac even though it was commanded by George Meade. Because Grant did, it came to be regarded as his army.

The Union commander's purpose in attacking Lee was to hold him in place, to keep him from maneuvering. Meanwhile, Sherman was to enter Georgia and then swing north to come into Lee's rear. In May of 1864 the offensive began.

On May 5, Grant and the Army of the Potomac collided with Lee and the Army of Northern Virginia. They met in the Wilderness, the scene of Lee's greatest triumph one year earlier, and the place of Stonewall Jackson's tragic fall. The area looked like a monster burial ground. Skeletal hands and legs lay everywhere. Bleached skulls of men

General Grant whittling on a stick during a lull in the Battle of the Wilderness, as sketched by a war correspondent.

78

A contemporary newspaper picture of the Battle of the Wilderness. Union soldiers move up to battle in the dense underbrush of the woods.

and horses with eyeless sockets seemed to stare from every bush.

The two-day Battle of the Wilderness was among the bloodiest of the war. It was a bitter struggle in which men grappled hand to hand amid burning forests. While the crackle of flames counterpointed the roar of battle and the screams of the stricken, U. S. Grant sat on a stump near Wilderness Tavern. He smoked cigars and whittled on a stick, calmly feeding in division

after division in an effort to overwhelm Lee.

Marse Robert did not give, although at one point his lines were in such danger of collapsing that he rode forward on Traveler to lead a charge himself. But then reinforcements arrived, and the men persuaded General Lee to go to the rear while they rushed forward to save the day.

The battle ended in a stand-off. There were terrible casualties, however—between 15,000 and 18,000 killed and wounded for the Union, between 7,750 and 11,400 for the Confederacy. If casualties were to measure success, then Lee would surely be judged the victor. But casualties measure only the costs of the battle. What had happened at the Wilderness was that Grant had succeeded in holding Lee in place. He had prevented the Confederate commander from maneuvering against him, as Lee had maneuvered against so many Union generals before.

True enough, Grant's army had suffered grievously. Because it did suffer so, and was to suffer more, the false legend of "Grant the butcher" was born. In truth, however, Grant was on the offensive, and the offensive usually has higher casualties than the defensive. Moreover, he was attacking the King of Spades. It is doubtful if any of the great generals in history could have moved against an entrenched Marse Robert without taking the greater losses. Finally, Grant had a force twice the size of Lee's and could therefore afford to lose more men.

So the struggle between the two armies became a conflict between Grant the slugger and Lee the boxer. Grant was willing to take losses in the hope that sooner or later Lee would drop his guard and Grant could land the knockout blow. Again and again, Grant tried to get around Lee's right flank, or to lure him out of his fortifications. Each time Grant sideslipped to his left, Lee fell back to his right to confront the Federal Commander. That was how they struggled south through the Wilderness. Then, after the fourth attempt was foiled at the Battle of Cold Harbor—a blood bath for the Federal troops—Grant made his great decision. He decided to attack Lee's rear.

Here was an audacity worthy of Marse Robert himself. And the daring maneuver was brought off with a skill and timing equally masterful. Before Lee knew what had happened, Grant's army had moved all the way down to the James River. He menaced Lee's source of supply. If he could get into Petersburg, he would seal Lee's doom. Petersburg, however, did not fall—and Lee rushed there just in time to save the city. Thwarted once again, Grant settled down to besiege Petersburg.

Robert E. Lee had said a siege would make defeat for him a "mere question of time." And here he was, cooped up in Petersburg, while all around him Confederate fortunes were falling. Several hundred miles to the southwest, General William Tecumseh Sherman had captured Atlanta and was preparing to begin his famous (or infamous) "march through Georgia" to cut off Lee's food supply and weaken the South's will to fight. More than a hundred miles to the northwest of Petersburg, General Grant had sent Phil Sheridan into the Valley of the Shenandoah on a similar mission of destruction.

The Valley was one of the South's

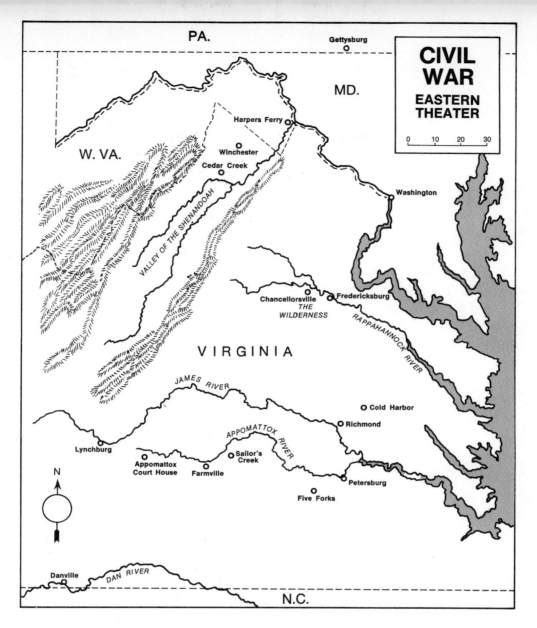

CIVIL WAR
EASTERN
THEATER

0 10 20 30

PA.

Gettysburg

MD.

W. VA.

Harpers Ferry

Winchester
Cedar Creek

Washington

VALLEY OF THE SHENANDOAH

Chancellorsville
THE
WILDERNESS

Fredericksburg

RAPPAHANNOCK RIVER

VIRGINIA

JAMES RIVER

Cold Harbor

Richmond

APPOMATTOX RIVER

Lynchburg

Appomattox
Court House

Sailor's
Creek

Farmville

Petersburg

Five Forks

N

Danville

DAN RIVER

N.C.

great assets. It provided food and forage for Lee's army. It was also a dagger aimed at the Federal heart in Washington. Because the Valley ran downward from southwest to northeast, a Rebel army marching down it was a threat to Washington. Again and again, Lee had sent Stonewall Jackson and others marching down the Shenandoah. Each time, they so frightened Washington that Union troops were drawn back from southeastern Virginia to defend the Federal capital.

It might almost be said that the clever Lee defended his own capital of Richmond in the Valley of the Shenandoah more than a hundred miles away.

U. S. Grant knew this. He wanted to seize the Valley and to "eat out Virginia clear and clean so that crows flying over it for the balance of the season will have to carry their provender with them." Such a decision would have cruel effects. Yet, as General Sherman told the people of Atlanta: "War is cruelty, and you cannot refine it." And so, short Phil Sheridan led Federal troops up into the Shenandoah Valley. They burned barns and fields and they slaughtered cattle. Billowing clouds of smoke shut out the sun by day, and the night was brightened with the glow of burning buildings.

Alarmed, Lee sent Jubal Early into the Valley to drive Sheridan away. But even "Old Jube" was not up to this assignment. He came close to victory at Cedar Creek, attacking while the Union general was 20 miles away in Winchester. But then Sheridan made his famous ride to the battlefield, rallying his troops as he rode among them on his splendid warhorse, Rienzi, and turning defeat into victory. After that, the Valley was closed to the South forever.

Denied his sources of supply in the Shenandoah, menaced in his rear by Sherman marching north through the Carolinas, Robert E. Lee began the spring of 1865 by preparing for a daring breakout dash from Petersburg.

General Lee's plan was to join forces with General Joe Johnston, who was slowly retreating north before

General Sheridan on Rienzi, riding to battle at Cedar Creek.

Sherman. Then he and Johnston would overwhelm Sherman, after which they would turn north to destroy Grant.

To break out of Petersburg, Lee hoped to capture Fort Stedman and thus open an escape hole in the Union line. On March 25, 1865, the Rebels attacked Stedman in a silent rush. They seized it. Now, if they could widen this breakthrough, Lee's whole army could pour east through the gap. But the Federals rallied. They retook Stedman. Then it was Grant's turn.

Grant was ready to strike hard at Lee's right, and thus cut off the Confederate escape route south. On March 29, a full Union corps hit the Rebel right, while fiery little Phil Sheridan led another corps of cavalry and one of infantry still farther below it. Sheridan wanted to get to a place called Five Forks, and thus to attack Lee from the rear. But Lee countered by sending General George Pickett to Five Forks.

On April 1, Sheridan ordered an attack on Pickett, crying, "This battle must be fought and won before the sun goes down!"

As his lines swept forward, the Rebel guns struck at them. Seeing his soldiers falter, Sheridan rode toward them.

"Come on," he cried, swinging his little flat cap. "Go at 'em! Move on with a clean jump, or you'll not catch one of them!"

A soldier beside him was hit in the throat. "I'm killed!" he cried, blood spurting from the wound.

"You're not hurt a bit!" Sheridan yelled. "Pick up your gun, man, and move right on!"

Instantly obeying, the soldier trotted forward—and fell dead.

Now the blue lines were going forward. Sheridan seized his little swallow-tailed battle flag from his color sergeant and rode up and down his lines. A bullet pierced the flag and another killed the color sergeant. Still, Sheridan rode Rienzi in full view of his troops and the enemy. Spurring his black mount forward, he led a charge on the Rebel position. He went over the works in a soaring jump, and the infantry swarmed in after him.

Victory was near, and Sheridan was eager to seize it. He could in effect end the war that day by winning the Battle of Five Forks—and he knew it. Urging his soldiers ahead, he roared, "I want you men to understand we have a record to make before the sun goes down that will make Hell tremble!"

At last, Pickett's force was scattered. Five Forks fell to Sheridan. Now, with Lee's flank turned, Grant struck next day at his center.

Federal artillery hurled a horrible weight of metal upon the Confederate positions outside Petersburg. Then line after line of Federal infantry rose up and moved forward. Gaining momentum, they tore through the Rebel center. Alarmed, Lee sent A. P. Hill to plug the gap, but the gallant Rebel general took a bullet in the heart. Having already lost Jeb Stuart as well as

General Robert E. Lee, on Traveler.

Jackson, the Confederate commander wept to lose still another of his lieutenants. Then he called upon the usually reliable James Longstreet. This times, however, "Old Pete" could not hold the Federals, and Lee prepared to abandon Petersburg.

He hoped to get to Danville, the city on the Dan River to which President Jefferson Davis had begun moving the Confederate capital, now that Richmond had to be abandoned. Perhaps

Lee could still refresh and resupply his ragged army of 30,000 veterans, and still make junction with Joe Johnston's army to the south. Although it was a forlorn hope, Robert E. Lee clung to it with all the tenacity of his indomitable will.

But U. S. Grant was also tenacious, and he was pursuing Lee as doggedly as a bulldog. Federal cavalry were everywhere, nipping at Lee's heels. Behind them marched three corps of Union infantry. The soldiers in blue were high-hearted and stepping high in their eagerness to end the war. Without food and almost without hope, Lee's weary veterans stumbled on. On April 6, the Federals caught up with them at a place called Sailor's Creek. They captured most of Lee's wagons and nearly broke his army. Seated on Traveler, Marse Robert saw the wreck of shattered Rebel regiments back-washing around him.

"My God," he cried out in anguish, "is the Army dissolved?"

It was not completely gone, but Lee lost between 7,000 and 8,000 men that day. That night, after desertions and surrenders by men who could fight no more, the Army of Northern Virginia was down to 15,000 men. Hurrying relentlessly after them were Grant's 80,000 Federals.

On April 7, Lee and his splendid scarecrows staggered into Farmville, where they received their first rations in five days. Lee still had hopes. He might yet reach Danville.

Receiving a note from Grant inviting him to surrender, he handed it to Longstreet, who read it and said, "Not yet."

Now the destination was Appomattox Station, where four food trains were waiting. From Appomattox, Lee could march to Lynchburg and then swing south to Danville and safety.

But Sheridan's horsemen and foot soldiers were gaining. They brushed past Lee's southern flank and swept into Appomattox Station. There they captured Lee's precious supply trains and put themselves across his line of march. That night, the Army of Northern Virginia stumbled into Appomattox Court House. Below them, Lee knew, was Sheridan's force. Yet, if it were only cavalry, Lee might still burst through. If Sheridan also had infantry, however, all was lost.

April 9, 1865, was Palm Sunday. Robert E. Lee began it by putting on a new gray uniform. From a sash of deep red silk hung the jeweled sword he had been given by ladies in England. Red-stitched spurred boots were on his feet, and his hands were covered by long gray gauntlets.

"I have probably to be General Grant's prisoner," Marse Robert explained to his officers, "and I thought I must make my best appearance."

Even then, Lee still had hopes. Down toward Sheridan charged a line of desperate butternuts. They burst through Sheridan's cavalry screen— and saw the solid blue lines of Union infantry.

It was all over.

After four bloody years, the Army of Northern Virginia had come to the end of the road. Lee knew it and said, "Then there is nothing left for me to do but to go and see General Grant, and I would rather die a thousand deaths!"

Below him, Phil Sheridan was in a rage of impatience. He feared to see the prize slip from his grasp. Massing his men and his horse, he cried, "Now

Northern officers receive the Confederates' flag of truce.

smash 'em, I tell you, smash 'em!"

Just as bugles blew the attack, a lone rider galloped out from the Confederate lines. He carried a flag of truce, and informed General Sheridan that General Lee awaited General Grant in the McLean House.

Suspicious of a trick at first, Sheridan finally ordered a cease-fire. A strange quiet came upon the rival hosts at Appomattox. The men relaxed on their guns. Some picked flowers. Dazed, they listened to the song of birds. Then General Grant rode up. There was mud on his private's blouse. His face above the brown beard was strained, for he had a bad headache and had been up all night bathing his feet in hot water and applying mustard plasters to his wrists and neck.

Grant inclined his head toward the McLean House and asked Sheridan, "Is General Lee up there?"

Sheridan replied, "Yes."

Grant said, "Well, then, let's go up."

Robert Edward Lee sat inside the McLean House with two aides. Grant came in alone. The two generals shook hands, each man aware of the contrast in their appearance, but neither giving any sign of it. Some of Grant's officers entered the room to stand behind Grant, seated at a table opposite Lee. For a few minutes, Grant and Lee chatted about their experiences in Mexico.

Then Lee said, "I asked to see you to ascertain upon what terms you would receive the surrender of my army."

Grant quickly outlined his terms. Then he put them in writing.

Lee asked about the horses of his men, pointing out that they were their private property.

Grant promised "to let all the men who claim to own a horse or mule take the animals home with them to work their little farms."

"This will have the best possible effect on the men," Lee said. "It will be very gratifying and will do much toward conciliating our people."

Even then Robert Edward Lee real-ized that the South had been defeated. Even though it was merely the Army of Northern Virginia that he was surrendering, he knew that the Confederacy could not survive such a blow. Combat might sputter on, as it did for six weeks more, but the soul of the South expired on that fateful Palm Sunday of 1865.

Signing the surrender, General Lee arose. He shook hands with Grant. He bowed to the others and strode out the door. Pausing on the porch of the Mc-Lean House, he drew on his gauntlets. Tears came to his eyes as he gazed in sorrow toward the hillside where his little army rested, brave and loyal to the last. Twice driving his gloved fist into his palm in savage regret, Robert Edward Lee swung aboard Traveler and rode away.

SANTIAGO
The Land-Sea Fight
That Humbled Spain

For more than a century the young American nation had followed George Washington's advice to avoid "the broils of Europe." However, as the 1800s came to a close, the United States began to look outward.

Powerful voices began to clamor for an "American empire." Businessmen declared that they needed new markets to absorb the surplus manufactures of the mushrooming American industry. It was maintained that if America did not join the imperialist powers of Europe then expanding at the expense of Asia and Africa, she would be left behind. Captain Alfred Thayer Mahan, author of writings regarded as the "bible" of sea power, declared: "We must come out of our isolation, which a hundred years ago was wise and imperative, and take our share in the turmoil of the world."

Gradually the habit of thought in the United States began to change. Of

88

course Americans did not suddenly decide that they wanted to be like the French and British and set up a chain of overseas colonies by force of arms. But they did question isolation. For the first time, Americans began to doubt that they could get along without the rest of the world.

As they did, Cuba revolted against Spain.

Cuba was the "pearl of the Antilles." Columbus discovered the island in 1492, and the Spanish flag had flown there since 1511. From Cuba had sallied forth many of those expeditions which brought European civilization to the southern part of North America and to all of Latin America. But after the Napoleonic Wars had weakened the power of Spain, her New World colonies began to break away from her one by one.

In 1868 Cuba rebelled. But the rebellion was put down in a bloody ten-year war. Thereafter Spanish rule grew oppressive. It was not intended to be cruel or unjust, but a bumbling administration had exactly those effects. In 1895 Cuba rose once more against Spain.

This time, many Cuban patriots came to New York City. There they played skillfully on American sympathy for any revolution that might resemble their own. Stories of Spanish atrocities were widespread. In truth, there was much cruelty on both sides. But it was the voice of the Cuban patriots that was heard in America, and

Cuban rebels near Santiago de Cuba during the ten-year war against the Spanish.

it was trumpeted throughout the land by the sensational "yellow press."

By the end of the nineteenth century, the daily newspapers had become a power in world affairs. At that time, their standards of accuracy were not quite what they are today. Some newspapers of the yellow press were shamelessly sensational. They would print the wildest tales merely to sell newspapers. In New York, the nation's news capital, none was more shameless than Joseph Pulitzer's *World* or the *Journal* of William Randolph Hearst.

When the Cuban Revolution broke out, the *World* and the *Journal* were engaged in a bitter battle to sell newspapers. Both seized upon the Cuban Revolution as a source of the kind of exciting story that would help sell their papers. Neither worried too much about the truth of the tales that they printed. They were delighted by any report that would portray the Spaniards as cruel, swarthy, cowardly oppressors—the old caricature of the Spanish people which the Americans inherited from England. It was untrue, of course, as are all such attempts to besmirch an entire people. But this made no difference to Pulitzer or Hearst.

When an artist cabled the *Journal* that there would be no war and he wished to return home, Hearst replied, "Please remain. You furnish the pictures, and I'll furnish the war." In other words, he would do anything to

bring one on, even if it included his own country.

Meanwhile Pulitzer's *World* printed reports such as this: "Blood on the roadsides, blood on the fields, blood on the doorsteps, blood, blood, blood! The old, the young, the weak, the crippled—all are butchered without mercy. . . . Is there no nation wise enough, brave enough, to aid this blood-smitten land?"

Thus the two publishers tried to draw their nation into the conflict on the side of the Cuban revolutionaries. Even though their influence was enormous and the American people did sympathize with the Cubans, Pulitzer and Hearst probably would not have succeeded by themselves. A warmongering press, even one assisted by the new spirit of imperialism, was simply not enough to persuade the nation to take up arms.

This was because America generally does not fire the first shot. She must be provoked into war, as President Polk well knew in the dispute with Mexico. Moreover, Spain was most anxious to avoid hostilities with the United States. When President William McKinley sent the battleship *Maine* right into Havana harbor during a riot there, Spain barely protested. Yet Spanish authorities realized that *Maine's* presence in Cuban waters might trigger an incident that would cause a war.

"We are trying to avoid this at any cost," they informed McKinley.

Spanish fears were justified. On the

The Maine *blows up in Havana harbor.*

night of February 15, 1898, a terrible explosion shook *Maine* and sent her to the bottom with 250 American seamen. It is still not known who sank the *Maine*. Spain was the least likely suspect, but it was Spain whom most Americans blamed.

In New York, William Randolph Hearst heard the news, and told an editor, "This means war."

Unfortunately he was right. Although Spain acceded to every American request except the impossible demand of outright Cuban independence, President McKinley still asked Congress for power to intervene in Cuba. On April 19, 1898, Congress declared Cuba free and independent, demanded Spanish withdrawal from the island and granted McKinley the power to achieve both objectives. On April 21, Spain broke off diplomatic relations with the United States, and on April 25 Congress declared that a state of war had existed since that day.

Because the Spanish-American War was basically a naval war, it was the first and only conflict for which America was prepared. In 1898 the United States Navy was among the world's finest. It was three times as large as Spain's and far more up-to-date and efficient. This was because Captain Mahan's theory of an imperialist America backed by a strong navy had

Commodore Dewey on the bridge of his flagship at Manila Bay. The Spanish fleet burns in the background.

had a powerful influence on the government. Mahan's chief convert was Theodore Roosevelt, the Assistant Secretary of the Navy. Thus America was in excellent position to duel Spain in both the Pacific and the Atlantic.

The first blows were struck in the Philippines. Here Commodore George Dewey sailed right into Manila Bay to challenge the Spanish fleet there. For the last time Spain's historic red-and-orange battle flags were flung up to the Pacific winds. For the last time Spanish shot went screaming toward a Pacific foe. This time, the shots were

high. A shell burst above *Olympia,* Commodore Dewey's flagship.

He said calmly to the ship's captain, "You may fire when ready, Gridley."

Olympia's starboard eight-incher gushed flame and smoke. Then all five American cruisers were firing. Ship by ship, they battered the seven vessels of the Spanish fleet. Five times they promenaded past the enemy, three times west and twice east, bellowing as they passed—and in the end the Spanish fleet was destroyed.

In seven hours it was all over. In that short space of time Dewey's squadron became the master of Manila and all the Philippine Islands. With not a man killed and only eight lightly wounded, the United States had become a world power and an imperialist nation. She had evicted Spain from the vast blue ocean that the great Spanish navigators had charted and named, and she had begun her own long Asiatic career.

Even though the Battle of Manila Bay was to have great and lasting consequences, Commodore Dewey's victory was still a sideshow to the war in Cuba. Here the American objective was to free the island from Spanish rule. A blockade of Cuban ports was begun while an invasion force to capture Havana was collected. But then one of Spain's two Atlantic fleets sailed for Cuba to break the blockade.

This sea force, the larger of the two fleets, was commanded by Admiral Pascual Cervera. It consisted of four outdated cruisers and a few destroyers and torpedo boats. As Cervera crossed the ocean, he began to run low on coal. So he sailed into Santiago de Cuba, one of the few ports still open to Spanish ships. Here Cervera hoped to refuel his ships and then put to sea again. Here, however, he was overtaken by Rear Admiral William Sampson with a powerful fleet of battleships, cruisers and smaller vessels. Sampson immediately bottled up Cervera in Santiago harbor.

Now the whole American plan of battle changed. Admiral Sampson dared not sail into Santiago as Dewey had stormed Manila Bay. The port's shore batteries were much too strong for that, and there is an old nautical saying: "A ship is a fool to fight a fort." Neither could Sampson sail away and permit Cervera to sally forth and perhaps intercept and sink the American expedition to Havana. Therefore, if Cervera's fleet could not be menaced from the sea, it had to be attacked from the landward side.

On May 29, the War Department cabled General William Shafter in Tampa, Florida: "YOU ARE DIRECTED TO TAKE YOUR COMMAND ON TRANSPORTS . . . TO THE VICINITY OF SANTIAGO DE CUBA . . . TO CAPTURE OR DESTROY THE GARRISON THERE; AND . . . WITH THE AID OF THE NAVY CAPTURE OR DESTROY THE SPANISH FLEET."

William Shafter was an old Indian fighter who had literally waxed fat after leaving the frontier for the East. He weighed 300 pounds and needed to stand on a box to mount his horse. Brave and determined, General Shafter was nevertheless not experienced in handling large bodies of troops.

Nor was the U.S. Army prepared for war. While the Navy was being modernized and strengthened, the ground forces had again been so neglected that in 1897 there were only 25,000 American soldiers under arms. This force, representing a U.S. population of 73,000,000, was probably in proportion of soldiers to civilians the tiniest army on the globe.

True enough, in 1898 Congress did raise its strength to 62,000 men. But this was still about 70,000 men less than the Spanish Army. Moreover, the U.S. Army was never able to reach its authorized strength. This was because President McKinley had issued a call for 125,000 volunteers—and most able-bodied Americans preferred the easier discipline of the volunteer units to the hard drill of the regular Army. Actually, the arrival of the high-spirited, untrained volunteers in the various camps across the nation only served to complicate the Army's problems of forming an efficient fighting force.

General Shafter's camp at Tampa was one of the most disorganized. There were shortages of rifles, food, clothing and ammunition. There was not enough shipping space. Boxcars arriving at the camp had no signs on the outside to distinguish one from another. An officer looking for bullets would open a car and find patent-leather shoes. Volunteers were often seen begging for food in the streets while boxcars full of food rotted on unknown railroad sidings outside of town.

The best that could be said for the entire military situation was that the Americans were well armed. They had the excellent Krag-Jorgensen rifle firing from a five-shot magazine, the Gatling machine gun and some good horse-drawn artillery. Nevertheless, when General Shafter's 18,000 men set sail from Tampa, they went to sea as a catch-as-catch-can invasion force. No one assigned this unit to that transport, so that ships were literally "seized" by regimental commanders on a first-come-first-served basis. Colonel Theodore Roosevelt, who had resigned as Assistant Secretary of the Navy, actually took a squad of Rough Riders to hold a transport against another regiment. Finally, the tangle of men, horses and equipment was unraveled. On June 14, the Americans sailed for Cuba.

Enroute, General Shafter decided against trying to storm Santiago's land defenses. Instead, he would land his army 15 miles east of the city at a place called Daiquirí. Then he would advance overland on the city.

On June 22, 1898, the landings began.

Lieutenant General Arsenio Linares had about 36,000 troops holding the Province of Santiago. Of these, about 12,000 held the city itself. If General Linares had decided to defend his command at the water's edge, he might have given the *Yanquis* a bloody check. Only a few hundred men posted on the high cliffs of Daiquirí could have turned the sea red with American blood. But not a Spanish shot was fired as the American transports dropped anchor and warships blasted the empty Daiquirí cliffs with big guns.

Soon bobbing boats loaded with doughboys in blue began rowing ashore. Cheering wildly, the boats raced each other. They came in un-

The skirmish at Las Guasimas.

opposed, greeted by ragged Cuban revolutionaries.

"Vivan los Americanos!" they cried. "Long live the Americans!"

Back came the shouts: *"Viva Cuba libre!* Long live a free Cuba!"

Delighted, the Cubans flashed white grins beneath their drooping black mustaches and immediately began asking for cigarettes.

Out at sea, horses were "landed" by throwing them overboard. Then cavalry buglers standing on the shore blew the calls that turned them in the right direction and started them swimming for dry land. By nightfall a force of 6,000 American soldiers with all their equipment had landed safely in Cuba at a loss of only five horses drowned.

Now the Yankee invaders turned their faces westward and began advancing on Santiago. Blundering through the dense jungle, tormented by clouds of mosquitoes, perspiring in the intense heat, Americans softened by shipboard life kept plodding doggedly onward. The Spaniards fell back, fighting delaying actions as they did. Behind them, General Linares was strengthening the city's defenses. At a place called Las Guasimas, the two forces fought a brief battle that resulted in 16 Americans killed and 52 wounded against Spanish losses of 10 dead and 18 wounded. Obviously, the despised "Dons" could fight.

Still the Americans pressed on. Their pace slackened, however, when

General Shafter became prostrated by the heat. Then he developed gout and had to waddle about with his foot swathed in a gunny sack, unable to get his huge body aboard a horse. Meanwhile, General Linares continued to make his position stronger. His men dug rifle pits on San Juan Heights and fortified the little village of El Caney to the left or north of San Juan. There they sat in their straw sombreros and sweat-stained blue coats, calmly awaiting the *Yanquis*.

Shafter attacked them by sending one division to the right against El Caney and its little stone fort, and then moving against San Juan Heights with the rest of his command two hours

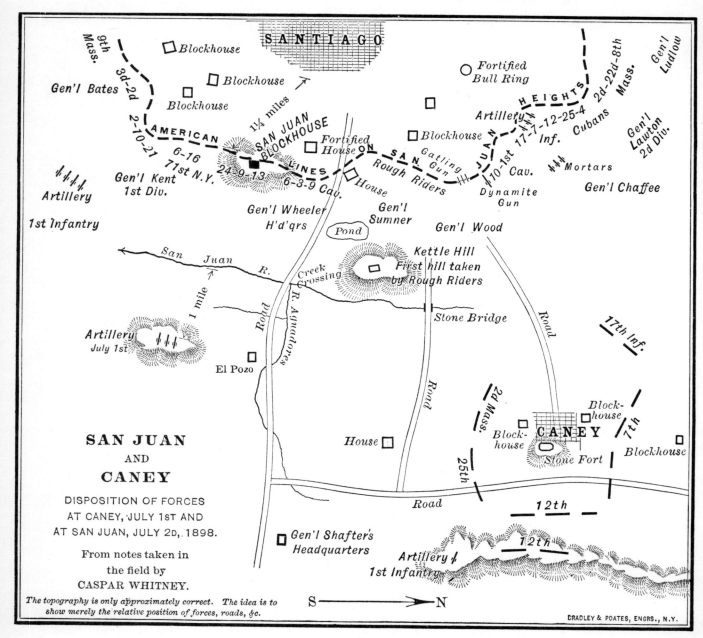

SAN JUAN
AND
CANEY

DISPOSITION OF FORCES
AT CANEY, JULY 1ST AND
AT SAN JUAN, JULY 2D, 1898.

From notes taken in
the field by
CASPAR WHITNEY.

The topography is only approximately correct. The idea is to show merely the relative position of forces, roads, &c.

S ——→ N

BRADLEY & POATES, ENGRS., N.Y.

later. At first, the Spaniards at El Caney held out stubbornly. Gradually, however, the Americans closed in. About 150 yards from the fort, a call for sharpshooters was issued. Thirty or forty crack shots crept forward. They took aim at every visible rifle pit, window, door or gunport. Under that steady, killing fire, the Spaniards at last collapsed—and El Caney fell to the Americans.

On the American left the attack against San Juan moved ahead in confusion. Yankee artillery fired black-powder ammunition that sent up clouds of smoke and gave away their position. Replying with smokeless powder, the Spaniards silenced the American guns. Then the Spaniards shot down an American observation balloon. Marking the spot where it fell, they directed all their fire on the spot and panicked an entire regiment of volunteers. Regular soldiers were sent to the spot. Their spearhead was a regiment of dismounted Negro cavalrymen led by Lieutenant John J. ("Black Jack") Pershing. Next came the Rough Riders, led by Teddy Roosevelt. Because of the roughness of the terrain, all the troopers, Negro and white, were dismounted. Their mission was to take Kettle Hill, on the right of San Juan. They went up to the slope with a rising cheer. They quickly cleared the area of Spaniards and pressed on to seize high ground to the rear.

But on their left, at San Juan Hill, the Americans were being pinned down by Spanish gunfire. Then a lieu-tenant named John Parker brought up a battery of three Gatling machine guns. The famous "coffee grinders" began to hammer away, driving the Spaniards out of their trenches. With that, the American troops rose up and launched the celebrated "Charge at San Juan Hill."

It was not actually a continuous charge. It was a combination creep-run-and-fall, made in the face of savage enemy fire. Foreign military observers watching it thought it was unwise. "It is very gallant, but very foolish," one of them said.

Nevertheless, the sweating men in blue pressed steadily up San Juan. Rattled by the Americans' slow, silent ascent, the Spaniards began firing high. Coming in under this wild fire, the doughboys joined forces and routed the enemy.

Now General Linares' outer defenses were in American hands. General Shafter called upon the Spanish commander to surrender. Before he received a reply, Admiral Cervera in Santiago harbor made a bold bid to escape.

The defeat at San Juan had convinced Admiral Cervera that he had better make a dash for freedom before the Americans captured the city and his fleet as well. On the morning of July 3, 1898, his ships began moving out of the harbor.

Cervera's flagship *Maria Teresa* led. Next came the cruisers *Vizcaya, Cristóbal Colón* and *Oquendo,* followed by the destroyers *Pluton* and *Furor.* Out-

97

Above: U.S. cavalrymen come charging up Kettle Hill. Below: Reaching the top of San Juan Hill, American soldiers capture the San Juan block house.

side the harbor, the American fleet was on routine patrol. No one suspected that Cervera would try to break out. In fact, Admiral Sampson had sent the battleship *Massachusetts* and the smaller *Suwanee* to fuel at the new base the Marines had captured at Guantánamo Bay. Then on the very day Cervera chose to escape, the admiral had sailed east in his flagship *New York* to confer with General Shafter.

The winding, narrow and shallow channel was partially blocked by a sunken American ship. Admiral Cervera's ships had to come out to sea slowly, ten minutes apart. Aboard *Maria Teresa,* Captain Victor Concas ordered the bugles blown for battle.

"The sound of my bugles was the last echo of those which history tells us were sounded at the capture of Granada," Concas said. "It was the signal that the history of four centuries of grandeur was at an end, and that Spain was becoming a nation of the fourth class." Glancing at Admiral Cervera, Captain Concas murmured, "Poor Spain!"

The admiral looked away, and *Maria Teresa* came slowly out to battle.

Startled at first, the Americans quickly recovered. Their guns began bellowing. A converging fire fell on *Maria Teresa.* The ship shuddered and swung to the west or right. It headed straight for the cruiser *Brooklyn,* the most westward American ship. Cervera hoped to knock out *Brooklyn*

and thus open a gap through which his remaining ships might escape. But the American gunfire was too much for him, and Cervera ordered his flag cruiser beached. As he did, Admiral Sampson in *New York* heard the thunder of naval gunfire and turned the battleship around.

Now *Vizcaya* and *Colón* were out on the open sea. Taking advantage of the attention paid to *Maria Teresa,* the two ships swept away to a good lead. *Oquendo* sailing in their wake suffered the opposite fate. Once again the Americans were able to concentrate, and they so battered *Oquendo* that she, too, was forced to run ashore. Last to sortie were the little destroyers *Pluton* and *Furor*—and they were literally blown apart by the big guns of the battleships *Texas, Iowa* and *Indiana.* Even *New York,* after her quick return, scored big-gun hits.

Two ships remained of Cervera's squadron. These were pursued by *Texas, Brooklyn* and the new battleship *Oregon,* mightiest ship of the U.S. fleet. Now the Americans were gaining. They were scoring hits, while the Spanish fire went high. Thick coils of greasy smoke settled on the American ships. Yet they pressed on, finally forcing *Vizcaya* to run ashore. Next was *Colón.* When *Oregon* straddled *Colón* fore-and-aft with two shells from her huge 13-inchers, *Colón's* colors came fluttering down her mast.

The American sailors cheered. Ship bands began playing "The Star-Spangled Banner." But aboard *Texas*

The last ship of Cervera's fleet, Cristobal Colón, *burns.*

Captain John Philip cried, "Don't cheer, men—the poor fellows are dying."

Soon the Yankee sailors were rescuing the Spanish enemy whom they had just been fighting, and with that the naval portion of the Battle of Santiago came to an end.

In the city itself, the Spanish hung on until it became clear that the situation was hopeless. On July 17, 1898, they surrendered. Shortly afterward, another American expedition captured Puerto Rico without a fight.

Stunned, Spain sued for peace. Sorrowfully, reluctantly, she agreed to terms whereby Cuba became free and Guam, Puerto Rico and the Philippines were ceded to the United States for $20 million. In signing, Spain declared: "This demand strips us of the very last memory of a glorious past and expels us . . . from the Western Hemisphere, which became peopled and civilized through the proud deeds of our ancestors."

Never again would the red-and-orange flag which Christopher Columbus had first brought from Spain fly in the New World.

BELLEAU WOOD
The Marines
Save Paris

The Spanish-American War had made America an imperialist nation (a condition which lasted until 1946, when the Philippines received their independence). Yet the United States had not become internationalist. Most Americans still thought that they could avoid "the broils of Europe." America did not belong to any alliance of nations banding together for military security.

These alliances were the curse of Europe. By the turn of the century that continent, the homeland of the world's great empires, had been divided into two great alliances. On one side was the Triple Alliance formed by Germany, Austria-Hungary and Italy. On the other was the Double Entente of France and Russia. Britain still remained aloof from both camps. So long as she did, she preserved the "balance of power." This means that whichever side she chose to join automatically became the stronger. As long as she joined neither, it appeared that the peace of Europe would be maintained.

Then Imperial Germany began an

Kaiser Wilhelm during German Army maneuvers in 1900.

economic war with Britain. Having rapidly industrialized, Germany was now eager to find new world markets. This brought her into conflict with Britain, the world's chief industrial nation. Under the boastful Kaiser Wilhelm, Germany also began to chal-

lenge Britain's supremacy upon the sea. In 1904 the kaiser publicly proclaimed himself "Admiral of the Atlantic Ocean." With this, Britain secretly became semi-attached to the Double Entente of France and Russia.

Then, in 1905, an unheard-of event occurred. Little Japan defeated giant Russia. For the first time an Asian nation had humbled a European power. This fact was to have great influence on the colonial peoples of Asia and Africa, an influence still evident in the rising nationalism of those regions. More immediately, however, Russia's defeat suggested to Germany that her eastern neighbor offered no threat to her. Therefore, the Germans concentrated their troops on their western border with France. This drove Britain, France's cross-Channel neighbor, still deeper into alliance with the French and Russians.

Now Europe was divided into two camps. Historically, Europe has never been able to keep the peace when only two rival forces confront one another. Worse, these two giant alliances were now armed to the teeth. Militarism, the second curse of Europe, had seized all the great nations like a fever.

All of them had huge conscript armies. War was now thoroughly "democratized." In peace or war, every able-bodied man had to wear his national uniform. After serving a certain number of years, the men were discharged into a reserve. Thereafter they drilled near their homes a few times a month and for a few weeks during the summer. Not until they reached middle age did these European men put aside their uniforms for good. As a result, each standing army of young men was backed up by an enormous, ever-growing army of reservists.

So the twin evils of alliances and militarism had turned Europe into a powder keg. All that was needed to explode it was a spark. This was provided on June 28, 1914, when the Austrian Archduke Francis Ferdinand and his wife Sophie were murdered in Sarajevo, capital of the Austrian province of Bosnia. Because the assassin came from neighboring Serbia, Austria demanded that Serbia make amends for the crime.

The Austrian demands, however, were deliberately harsh. Austria really wanted to gobble up Serbia. Now Russia, Serbia's friend, began mobilizing by putting herself on a war footing and ordering her reservists back to active duty. Germany called on Russia to stop mobilizing. Russia refused, and with that the two nations were at war. Thereafter, France and Britain came to Russia's side and Austria joined Germany.

The horrible conflict first called the Great War—and now known as World War I—had begun.

The outbreak of war in Europe horrified America. Because it was a war between two groups of great empires, it rapidly spread across the world. Continents were engulfed in the flames of war. Yet most Americans believed that their nation should stay out. Even if they favored one side or another, they still thought their own country should remain neutral. President Woodrow Wilson even asked his countrymen to remain neutral "in thought as well as in action."

However, this was not possible. America was a seagoing nation, and because of this she was caught in a crossfire between Britain and Germany. The situation was similar to the situation a century earlier, when Britain's war with Napoleonic France led her to impress American seamen, thus starting the War of 1812.

This time the offending nation was Germany, because of her undersea warfare. To counter the British blockade, the kaiser ordered his submarines to sink neutral ships found in British waters. They did, often striking without warning. On May 7, 1915, a German submarine torpedoed the British liner *Lusitania*. The ship sank in 18 minutes, taking with her 1,198 human beings, of whom 128 were American citizens.

The sinking of *Lusitania* infuriated the American people. Even though war with Germany did not come for two more years, this event ended American neutrality. The nation now hoped for an Anglo-French victory. Gradually, as the submarine warfare continued, the United States became more and more hostile to Germany. She also became more committed to the cause of the Allies (as Britain,

France and their partners were called) because she had loaned them great sums of money and was supplying them with food and arms.

For a while Germany tried to conciliate America. But then in February, 1917, the kaiser ordered a resumption of all-out submarine warfare. In reply, President Wilson broke off diplomatic relations with Germany. That same month, Wilson learned that the kaiser was trying to persuade Mexico to make war upon the United States. This was the final blow, aggravated on March 16 by the torpedoing of two American ships by German submarines. On April 6, 1917, the United States declared war on Germany.

Although American arms had been "democratized" during the Civil War, when both sides fielded conscript armies, the nation did not follow Europe's lead in establishing a peacetime draft. As a result, the United States was ill prepared for World War I. And because America was 3,000 watery miles from the battlefront, it was almost a year before American troops were in France in force.

Long before then, World War I had settled down to trench warfare. To escape each other's artillery, both sides had dug in. Opposing trench networks, often only a few hundred yards apart, ran like a zigzag scar for 400 miles from a corner of Belgium across France to the Swiss border. Again and again the rival generals had attempted to burst through the other's

trenches by "penetration." Guns by the thousands bombarded the enemy position, and then armies by the hundred thousands tried to break through. Each time, the result was a bloody defeat. Locked in a murderous stalemate, the nations were bleeding each other white.

This was because the Industrial Revolution's effect upon warfare, like that of the Democratic Revolution, was even greater than it had been in the Civil War. Mass armies now had even deadlier weapons with which to produce mass slaughter. Because of the development of the machine gun and other automatic weapons, the bullet was an even more bloodthirsty king of the battlefield. And the defense was invincible. Men in trenches protected by fields of barbed wire and firing weapons that poured out hundreds of bullets per minute simply could not be overrun.

Yet the generals did not understand this. Their lack of understanding resulted partly from another change in warfare, which may be called the Managerial Revolution. This was the application of modern business methods to the business of war. The sort of men who could run a big company or plan a railroad or draw up a budget were now more in demand than the colorful fire-breathers of old. Colorless administrators were now in charge, and a general was more apt to issue orders from an armchair in his office than from a saddle in the field.

These business-efficiency methods

Canadian soldiers leaving a front-line trench to go "over the top."

gradually led commanders to become more impersonal. Soldiers were so many ciphers, to be used or "expended" like the bullets they fired, as the occasion demanded. Cold and calculating, then, these generals continued to stuff their opponents' trenches with their own dead in an effort to achieve penetrations which the supremacy of the defense had made impossible. Because of this, France was a shambles and her soldiers so weary of war that they mutinied in 1917.

Into this situation came the American Expeditionary Force under General John J. Pershing. At once, the Allies besought General Pershing to turn his soldiers over to them. Marshal Ferdinand Foch, the Allied commander, did not want an American army. He just wanted American soldiers, who would be trained by the Allies and enrolled in their divisions. General Pershing refused. This iron-willed commander told Marshal Foch that his men would fight anywhere at anytime, but as an American army.

Marshal Foch (left) and General Pershing

There were some bitter words between the two men.

At that point, the Germans opened their win-the-war offensive. They believed that the spring of 1918 was the time to strike the decisive blows, and they struck so savagely that they were on the brink of bursting through.

Alarmed, Pershing went to Foch's headquarters and told him, "All that we have are yours. Use them as you wish."

Overcome, Foch accepted the offer. American divisions joined the battle that blunted the first blows of the German offensive.

But the Germans were not through. Probing for a soft spot, they found one in the Chemin des Dames sector northeast of vital Paris. Here, they had 42 divisions opposite only 16 weary and poorly positioned Allied divisions. Here, on May 27, behind a thunderous artillery barrage, the Germans attacked. Almost at once they tore a gaping hole in the center of the Allied line. Jubilant, the Germans poured through the gap. They crossed the vital Aisne River on bridges the fleeing Allies had neglected to destroy. The Germans swept on, wave after wave of soldiers in coal-scuttle helmets and gray uniforms. They had scored a major breakthrough. Nothing like this had happened on the Western Front since 1914—four years earlier—when the Germans were just barely denied Paris in the First Battle of the Marne.

But now the exultant Germans stood on the Marne again, only 56 miles from Paris. Once more, a frightened French government prepared to flee the capital. Across the Channel in London, worried British leaders wondered if they should withdraw their troops from France. For the second time in four years, the roads west from the Marne were flooded with the backwash of defeat.

Old men and women plodded woodenly along, followed by bewildered children. Other civilians rode, in carts and farm wagons, in pony traps and ancient barouches hitched to cows and oxen or worn-out horses. Every vehicle was piled high with household belongings or crates of chickens. Sheep and goats mingled in the throng, and here and there a farmer led a cow on a leash or a young widow pushed her baby in a perambulator.

Into that terrified throng, but heading toward the battlefront, came columns of tall men in khaki. Some were bareheaded. All held their heads high as they marched, their arms and shoulders swinging in a slow and easy rhythm.

The men were American Marines, moving toward the collapsing center of the Allied line.

The Marine Brigade of the U.S. 2nd Division was commanded by an Army officer, Brigadier General James G. Harbord. After his spearheads had come swinging out the Paris road, General Harbord was told by the French commander, "Have your men prepare entrenchments some hundreds of yards to rearward in case of need."

Harboard passed the order along to his brigade with the comment: "We dig no trenches to fall back on. The Marines will hold where they stand."

They stood, that fateful June 3, on the left or north side of the Paris-Metz road. On the other side was the 2nd Division's Doughboy Brigade, covering the area around Vaux. This was a "busy" sector, but the busiest and most critical of all along the entire Allied front was the area defended by Harbord's men. This was Belleau Wood.

The Bois de Belleau was a tiny hunting preserve of about one square mile. It was a tangle of trees and huge boulders crisscrossed by ravines. When the Marines took up their positions opposite it on June 3, it was filling up with Germans preparing to push farther down the Paris road. Ahead of them they drove the remnants of the broken French units.

Into the American position stumbled weary French soldiers. *"La guerre est finie,"* they mumbled. "The war is over."

Even the French officers were convinced that they had been defeated. Again and again they advised the Americans to pull back. One despairing major even wrote out an order for retreat. But when Captain Lloyd Williams saw it he countermanded it with the remark, "Retreat, hell! We just got here."

Although the gallant Captain Williams was later killed, his cry was immortal. It thrilled the Marines even then scratching out those shallow pits which were to be called "foxholes," and it was exactly expressive of how the Americans—soldiers and Leathernecks alike—disdained any thought of retreat. For more than a year, these men had been training for combat. Now they were approaching it for the first time, and they had no wish to evade it. They were eager to come to grips with the Germans, to show them what Americans could do.

They got their wish very soon. In late afternoon, the German artillery began bombarding the Marines. It was the worst shelling the Americans had experienced so far, and it lasted for a whole dreadful hour. Then the Germans attacked.

They came on in compact masses. Out of the wood they marched in two columns, confident of overrunning the

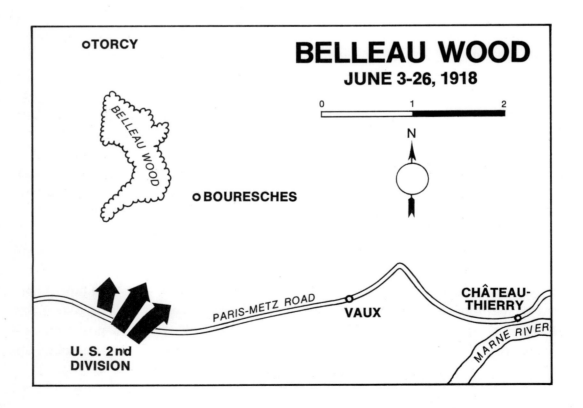

After a day's fight, roll call is taken in a camp near Belleau Wood.

Marines— if the bombardment had not already put the Americans to flight. The Marines watched their approach, waiting for them to come within range. Now the Marine tradition of expert, long-range marksmanship was to pay deadly dividends. At 300 yards, the enemy columns entered a waving field of green wheat—and the Marines opened fire.

Rifles popped and machine guns chattered, and German soldiers began to fall. Astonished by such long-range accuracy, the enemy columns still came on bravely. Then the American artil-lery began to roar. Shrapnel burst above the Germans' heads. Each time the smoke of the shell burst rolled away, the column beneath it was shorter and more ragged. Finally, the German columns broke. Enemy soldiers either dropped out of sight in the wheat or ran for the cover of the woods.

The following day and the next, the Germans returned to the attack. Again and again they struck at the American position, but that dreadfully accurate rifle and machine-gun fire backed up by artillery was too much for them every time. After three fruitless days, the German attacks were called off. Instead, the Germans began to dig in and fortify Belleau Wood.

Now it was the Marines' turn to attack.

On June 6 the Americans preparing to storm the mysterious dark bulk of Belleau Wood had no idea of what it contained. They could not know that it was swarming with Germans, cleverly positioned to take advantage of the wood's gloomy, jumbled terrain. Machine-gun nests were everywhere, usually concealed behind huge boulders protecting them like steel. In back of them were the riflemen and mortars. Nevertheless, the Marines attacked.

At dawn, they moved against high ground called Hill 142. They, too, passed through a green wheat field. A heavy dew shone on its leaves and the starry petals of blood-red poppies. Then the enemy artillery hit them. Still, they pressed on, only to be struck to the ground by Maxim machine-gun fire. Running among his men, Captain George Hamilton challenged each to go forward. Stung, they rose and charged the wood.

They came in with bared bayonets, yelling their high-pitched battle cry, "Eyah! Eyah!" They rushed the enemy machine guns with that glittering steel, bayoneting the Germans at their guns. The Marines took fearsome losses— but they also took Hill 142. Now in the late afternoon, with the high ground held, the main assault went forward.

In the center, gallant young Marine lieutenants stood erect. Each blew his whistle, pointed his officer's cane toward the wood, and cried, "Follow me!"

Hardly had the Americans started forward before the heavy Maxims began chugging. Once again the wheat was waving. Bullets, not wind, were moving it. Marines were cut to the ground, especially the officers leading the way. Sometimes the enemy fire was so deadly that whole platoons of Marines were compelled to hug the ground.

Gunnery Sergeant Dan Daly led one such platoon. A veteran of 25 years, a winner of the Medal of Honor and a man with a voice like a bullhorn, Sergeant Daly waved his bayoneted rifle over his head and roared, "C'mon, you sons of guns! Do you want to live forever?"

They did "come on," and many of them did not live.

On the right, the assault was less hurried. Some units attacked as though on parade. The Marines walked forward, saving their breath. They advanced in four waves, about 15 yards apart, each man five yards from the next man. These formations were also slashed and fragmented by the enemy fire. And they also pressed forward. On the extreme right Captain Donald Duncan was killed, and Lieutenant J. F. Robertson took command of his company.

"Come on, let's go," Robertson yelled, waving his pistol, and his Marines went into the wheat field toward the town of Bouresches.

Inside the field an enemy bullet caromed off Lieutenant Clifton Cates's helmet, knocking him down. Thinking him dead, his platoon moved on. But Cates was only stunned, with a dented helmet and a bloody lump on his head to testify to his good fortune. Recovering, he rejoined four of his men in a ditch. One of them named Tom Argaut took off his platoon leader's helmet to pour wine over the bloody lump.

"Dammit, Tom," Cates complained, "don't pour that wine over my head. Give me a drink of it."

Taking a good long swig, the lieutenant re-formed his men and with 30 Marines successfully took Bouresches.

Meanwhile, on the left flank a night assault had been ordered by General Harbord. The same battalion that had suffered so grievously taking Hill 142 was assigned to attack the village of Torcy near the extreme northern end of Belleau Wood. Once again, the Marines of this unit encountered misfortune. They were caught between heavy German fire on their right and fire from their own men on the left. One company was pinned down, its men on

Marine sharpshooters firing at long range in the woods.

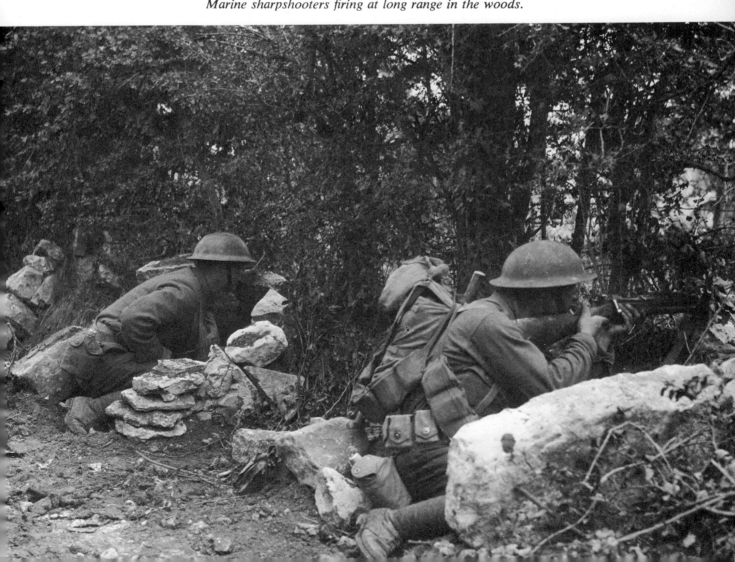

Wounded Americans receive emergency treatment in a first-aid station outside Belleau Wood.

the verge of panic, when Captain Lester Wass yelled for Lieutenant Gil Jackson.

"Yes, Captain," Jackson shouted back.

"Where are you?"

"Right here. Across the road."

"Stand up, so I can see you."

There was a pause, filled by the steady crackling of fire from friend and foe. Then came the voice of Lieutenant Jackson shouting, "Captain, if you want to see me, *you* stand up."

Smothered chuckles ran down the line of enlisted men, and in an instant a company of Marines on the verge of breaking had recovered its discipline. As dawn of June 7 broke, they crawled out of the field of fire.

Valorous as the assault of June 6 had been, it had not taken Belleau Wood. And it had gone forward at a cost of 1,087 American casualties, of whom 228 were killed. This was the worst single day of fighting the Marines would experience until Tarawa 25 years later. Yet, if the Marines had not yet succeeded in capturing their objective, they had saved Paris.

One day before they attacked, Premier Lloyd George of Britain had met with his military chiefs to discuss the "possibility of withdrawing the whole Army from France if the French crack." In Paris members of the Chamber of Deputies were clamoring for the dismissal of Marshal Foch. Thoroughly alarmed, the British and the French scheduled a high-level conference for June 7. That was the day after the news of the Marine assault had been received, and it was greeted with smiles of relief by the Anglo-French chieftains. They were outspoken in their praise of the Americans —not only the Marines at Belleau Wood but the Army units engaged elsewhere.

Nevertheless, all eyes remained focused on Belleau Wood. It was here that the German tide had been checked, and it was here that the Americans were now attempting to turn it back. Here, in other words, was the place where the troops of both nations had collided in significant battle. Because of the valor of the Americans, the French around them took heart and began to fight back themselves. As a result the German commander, General Erich Ludendorff, instructed his officers that the Americans must be stopped at all costs. On June 8, he told all army groups: "American units appearing on the front should be hit particularly hard in order to render difficult the formation of an American army."

Next day and for two days afterward, the Marines resumed the attack. Hammering up the long axis of Belleau Wood, they measured their advance by yards. Weary, hungry, their uniforms in tatters, they punched relentlessly forward. On June 12, with the help of a heavy artillery barrage, they broke through the third and final German line. Only a battered hunting lodge on the northern end of the line

Rounding up Germans by the hunting lodge in Belleau Wood. The fighting has blasted most

of the summer foliage from the trees.

remained in German hands.

Then, on the next night, the Germans counterattacked. They struck behind a barrage of shells and mustard gas. The Marines held their ground. Once again, they shocked the Germans with their marksmanship, repeatedly picking off enemy soldiers as far as 400 yards away. Never before had the Germans encountered such accuracy, and they reported to headquarters: "The enemy training in rifle marksmanship is remarkable. Once, as they broke through our left flank, they settled down behind rocks and by their rifle fire broke up every counterattack."

After the Germans were repulsed, the Marines began the grueling work of mopping up the wood. Then, to allow them to rest, they were relieved by the 7th Infantry Regiment of the U.S. 3rd Division. The Germans were not sorry to see them go, observing on June 16: "The various attacks by both the Marine Regiments were carried out with vigor and without consideration of losses. The moral effect of our firearms did not materially check the advance of the infantry. The nerve of the Americans is still unshaken. . . . The spirit of the troops is high and they possess an innocent self-confidence. A characteristic expression of the prisoners is 'we kill or get killed.' "

A week later, refreshed and reinforced, the Marine Brigade was back in Belleau Wood. On the night of June 23, attacking from their old positions, the Marines made their last attempt to evict the Germans. Tenacious as ever, the enemy clung to his last toehold in that ill-fated wood, now reeking with the smell of powder, gas and death. A daylight artillery barrage broke their will to remain, however, and on June 26 Major Maurice Shearer reported to General Harbord:

"WOOD NOW U.S. MARINE CORPS ENTIRELY."

So ended what one military historian has called a "local dogfight" in which the German commander had "staked all." As the battles of World War I are measured, Belleau Wood was hardly more than a skirmish. Yet, it occurred as the safety of Paris and the very outcome of the war hung in the balance. Will the Allies go down, the world wondered; can the Americans hold?

Not only did the Americans hold—at Vaux and Château-Thierry as well as Belleau Wood—but at Belleau Wood they went over to the attack. When they did, the hearts of the French and English everywhere along the line were lifted. When they did, they gained precious time in which Marshal Foch might regroup and re-organize for his own counterblows, the very strokes which were to win the war.

So it was not enough to echo Premier Georges Clemenceau's remark that Belleau Wood "saved Paris." It did even more—it gave the Allies back their will to fight.

No one was more aware of this than the French General Degoutte, who issued a special order: "In view of the brilliant conduct of the Marine Brigade, the General commanding the VIth Army orders that henceforth, in all official papers, the Bois de Belleau shall be named 'Bois de la Brigade de Marine.' "

From the German enemy came perhaps an even more eloquent testimony to the valor of those Americans whom they had met for the first time at Belleau Wood.

The Germans called them "devil dogs."

GUADALCANAL
The Battle
That Doomed Japan

Major General Alexander Vandegrift stood at the rail of the transport *McCawley,* squinting into the gathering darkness of August 6, 1942. Before and behind him steamed the ships carrying his 1st Marine Division to Guadalcanal. Far to the south sailed the aircraft carriers and gunfire ships that would bombard the island next morning.

General Vandegrift had to squint because he suffered from night blind-

ness. Yet he was pleased to see it get dark. This meant that he had slipped up on the Japanese unseen. For a week, now, the general had feared that the enemy's patrol planes might sight the American fleet. If they did, it could mean disaster for 89 American ships and 19,000 Marines.

Luckily, the skies had been overcast. Bad weather had grounded the Japanese airplanes. Because of this, the Americans had reached Guadalcanal undetected. Now, they were slipping past the island's "back door," the wild and uninhabited southern coast of the 90-mile-long island. In the morning they would be anchored off the northern coast, where the enemy had built an airfield. In the morning, General Vandegrift reflected, America would at last give Japan her answer to Pearl Harbor.

Realizing that it had turned completely dark and that he could not see at all, General Vandegrift called for an officer to assist him to his quarters. Up and down the fleet, bullhorns were bellowing: "Darken ship! The smoking lamp is out on all weather decks! All troops below decks!"

Soon silence came over the fleet. Marines in boots and battle dress fell asleep to the throbbing of ships' motors. In his cabin Alexander Vandegrift seized his pen and began to write a letter to his wife.

"Tomorrow morning at dawn," he wrote, "we land in the first major offensive of this war. Our plans have been made and God grant that our judgment has been sound. We have rehearsed the plans. The officers and men are keen and ready to go. Way before you read this you will have heard of it. Whatever happens you'll know that I did my best. Let us hope that best will be enough."

America was at war again because the Treaty of Versailles which ended World War I had actually led to World War II. The treaty, made in a spirit of vengeance, was harsh and unjust. It created chaos and resentment in Germany, so that it was easy for Adolf Hitler to make himself a dictator there. The Depression also helped Hitler. Hunger pangs sharpened the German sense of shame. Most Germans listened when Hitler, history's maddest Pied Piper, promised to restore their lost prosperity and prestige. So Germany began to rearm, in violation of the Versailles Treaty.

France and Britain should have tried to stop Hitler. The Allies, however, were distracted by the Depression. They were also so worried about the new menace of Communism that they tended to ignore the danger of Hitler and his fellow dictator, Benito Mussolini of Italy.

So Hitler and Mussolini grew bolder and bolder. They began to seize helpless countries. At last, when Hitler invaded Poland on September 1, 1939, the Allies moved to stop him—and World War II began.

At first the war was only between the Axis powers of Germany and Italy and the Allies of France and Britain. Russia, the United States and Japan stayed out of it. But then Hitler invaded Russia and forced the Russians to side with the Allies. Still America and Japan remained neutral. Although the Americans were in sympathy with the Allies, they thought they could "sit this one out." The actions of Japan, however, made this impossible.

Japan hoped to dominate the Far East. Even before World War II be-

The battleship Arizona *burning and sinking after the Japanese attack on Pearl Harbor.*

gan, she had invaded China. After the war broke out, Japan entered Allied colonies in Southeast Asia. Seeing how successful the German armies were, she joined the Axis. Now America became alarmed. Japan was notified that she must withdraw from Southeast Asia and China. Japan refused. Instead, she decided to attack America. While her envoys in Washington stalled for time, she secretly collected a fleet to make a surprise attack on Pearl Harbor.

Japan did not intend to conquer the United States. Even the fiercest of the generals and admirals who really ruled the country realized that this was not possible. The Japanese plan was merely to cripple America so that she could not interfere with Japanese conquest. Before America could recover from Pearl Harbor, Japan intended to protect her new empire with a chain of island outposts. Then, when the Americans did recover, they would be forced to fight a long, hard battle across the Pacific. Because the Japanese scorned the Americans as "soft," they believed that America would not be willing to launch such a long and bloody campaign. Instead, the Japanese thought, the Americans would be eager to settle for a peace that would leave Japan in possession of most of her stolen empire. Apparently, the Japanese were not impressed by the fact that America seemed to be preparing for war. Congress had already passed legislation providing for a "two-ocean navy," and in 1940 had established the first peacetime draft in American history.

So the Japanese did bomb Pearl Harbor, on December 7, 1941. They did sink most of the American Pacific Fleet, and they did cripple America. Then, striking savagely in every direction, they took Guam, Wake, the Philippines, the Dutch East Indies and Singapore. Supplanting the French in Indo-China, they also occupied Burma, Malay and Thailand. Mighty Britain, the old "Queen of the Waves," was chased from the Indian Ocean, and the Pacific became a Japanese lake.

Within six furious months, the Japanese had conquered what was the most populous and potentially the richest empire in history. Now they looked west toward India, toward a possible hookup with the Germans in the Middle East.

Now, also, the Japanese overreached. Blinded by their own success, they forgot their original plan. Instead of nailing down what they had seized, they reached out for more. They invaded the islands of the Southwest Pacific, where they ran into some resistance in the Battle of the Coral Sea. They even tried to take Midway Island from the United States, but at the Battle of Midway they suffered a disastrous naval defeat.

Yet the Japanese had lost none of their new lands. Still confident, they began to fortify their Pacific outposts. In the Solomon Islands, about 1,200 miles northeast of Australia, they began building an airfield at a place called Guadalcanal.

With dawn of August 7, 1942, General Vandegrift was again at the rail of *McCawley*. Although he no longer squinted, the corners of his eyes were wrinkled with worry. Overhead, Navy and Marine aircraft were bombing and strafing Guadalcanal and the little island of Tulagi across the channel. Both islands were wreathed in flame and smoke. To either side of *McCawley*, landing boats crowded with Marines ducking below the gunwales trailed long white wakes as they sped toward the landing beaches. Then came the report from Guadalcanal:

"Landing successful. No opposition."

General Vandegrift sighed in relief. The Japanese labor force employed on the Guadalcanal airfield had run into the jungle in terror the moment American bombs crashed among them.

Across the channel on Tulagi, however, the Japanese garrison stood its ground. Here, the short, stocky tan men in the mushroom helmets fought with dogged courage. The Marines had to use dynamite to blast them out of their caves and pillboxes. They had to do the same at the harbor islets of Guvutu-Tanambogo. By midday, however, the Marines had the upper hand.

But then the Japanese Air Force began counterattacking.

The enemy planes came winging down from Rabaul, the big air-sea base on the island of New Britain, about 600 miles to the northwest. They were "Betty" bombers escorted by Zero fighters. They hoped to sink the American transports then being unloaded in the channel. The Americans, however, were ready for them. They had been warned by the Coastwatchers—former islanders, mostly Australians, who had gone into hiding when the Japanese invaded their islands. From their lonely mountain outposts, the Coastwatchers kept watch on enemy ship and air traffic down the "Slot," the watery corridor which ran between the double chain of the Solomon Islands. Then they alerted the Americans by radio. On this day, their very first warning cleared the decks of ships for action and sent flights of fighters roaring aloft to await the enemy. Thus, when the Japanese came thundering over the channel, they were jumped by the "stacked" Americans and thumped by American antiaircraft power. As a result, 30 of 51 enemy planes were shot down.

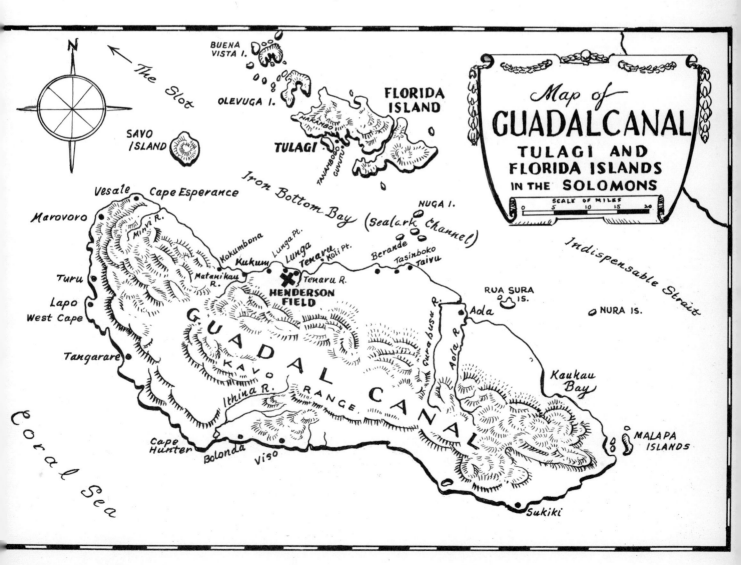

Flying so low that their reflections can be seen on the water, Japanese torpedo bombers go after American transports off Guadalcanal.

By nightfall, General Vandegrift was jubilant. His main body was safely ashore on Guadalcanal. The Americans had captured the airfield and renamed it Henderson Field in honor of a fallen Marine flyer. Over on Tulagi, the Marines broke an enemy night attack. Obviously, that island would soon fall. Vandegrift's only worry was the unloading operation. Supplies had begun to pile up on the Guadalcanal shore, making excellent targets for enemy aircraft. Next day, however, the second Japanese aerial strike still went for the transports.

Forty-five Bettys armed with torpedoes came in low over the water. They hoped to get below the level of the American guns, as they had done with British warships. But the American guns were built to fire low and had excellent fire-control systems. This time, the slaughter was even worse. American ships were showered with the debris of exploding Japanese planes. American sailors had to sweep their decks clear of the limbs and torsos of Japanese flyers. Nevertheless, the Japanese finally drew blood. The de-

stroyer *Jarvis* was crippled and eventually sunk, and the transport *George F. Elliott* was lost when an enemy plane crashed her amidships. Yet, of the 45 attacking planes, only one survived—and when its pilot arrived in Rabaul he proudly claimed that he had sunk a battleship!

Once again, Vandegrift was jubilant—until he learned that the aircraft carriers were withdrawing. Vice-Admiral Frank Jack Fletcher, in command of the carriers, feared to risk his two precious flattops to enemy submarine or torpedo-bomber attack. His withdrawal, however, meant that Vandegrift would lose his aerial support. It meant that Vice-Admiral Richmond Kelly Turner would also have to withdraw, taking still-unloaded transports with him. Vandegrift was thunderstruck. Without warning, his fortunes had flip-flopped. They fell even farther during the night of August 8–9.

Undetected by the Americans or the Coastwatchers, a Japanese fleet of cruisers and destroyers under Vice-Admiral Gunichi Mikawa had come stealing down the Slot. They slipped past Savo Island, the round island standing like a sentinel at the channel entrance. They sighted the American ships and Mikawa gave the order: "All ships attack!"

At once, Japanese torpedoes went hissing down their tubes to land splashing in the water and begin their deadly runs. Great gun barrels were rotated in the direction of their targets. Suddenly, the night silence was broken by the thunder of guns and exploding torpedoes. The darkness turned brilliant with cascading shells and the death fires of stricken American ships.

Admiral Turner's force had been completely surprised. Four of his cruisers—*Quincy, Vincennes, Astoria* and the Australian *Canberra*—were sunk. Luckily, Admiral Mikawa did not go after the transports, left as helpless as sheep deprived of their shepherds. Instead, he turned around and sped for the safety of Rabaul. Nevertheless, the Battle of Savo Island dealt the Americans a dreadful blow. In the clear daylight of August 9, Admiral Turner's remaining vessels departed from those waters which were soon to be known as Iron Bottom Bay because of the number of ships sunk there. Now Vandegrift had neither navy nor air cover nor many supplies.

He and his Marines were all alone.

Guadalcanal's sole value lay in Henderson Field. In fact, throughout the Pacific War the battle for the islands was actually a fight for island airfields. Control of the air meant control of the sea, and whoever could sail the sea without fear of enemy aircraft would win the war. Thus, Alexander Vandegrift was determined to hold Henderson Field. To do so, he formed his Marines around it in a defensive ring about 7,500 yards wide and 3,500 yards deep.

Up in Rabaul, Lieutenant General Haruyoshi Hyakutake was just as determined to retake Henderson Field. Moreover, he thought it would be easy, chiefly because he shared his countrymen's contempt for Americans as fighters. He also believed that there were only 2,000 Marines in the Guadalcanal area, when there were in fact 19,000. So he ordered Colonel Kiyono Ichiki to take his crack regiment down the Slot to oust the Americans.

At once, Colonel Ichiki boarded fast destroyers with 900 of his men and went speeding down the Slot. His remaining 1,000 soldiers followed in slower transports. Shortly after midnight of August 18, Colonel Ichiki and his men landed on Guadalcanal at a point 22 miles to the east of a Marine battalion holding the Tenaru River. Although Ichiki's orders instructed him to await the arrival of the rest of his regiment, the colonel decided not to do so. Even more than Haruyoshi Hyakutake, Kiyono Ichiki scorned the Americans. Surely 900 battle-tested Japanese soldiers would be more than enough for 2,000 soft Americans. So he predicted in his diary: "18 Aug. The landing. 20 Aug. The march by night and the battle. 21 Aug. Enjoyment of the fruits of victory."

By midnight of August 20, Colonel Ichiki had his men formed in a coconut grove opposite the Marines on the banks of the Tenaru. Actually, the Tenaru was not a river but a backwater. Where it should have emptied into the sea, it was blocked by a narrow sandspit. Across this sandspit came the soldiers of the Ichiki Detachment, howling "Banzai!" or "Hurrah!" and sprinting to close with the bayonet.

They were met by the yells and curses of the Marines, and by converging sheets of rifle and machine-gun fire that cut them to the ground. Again and again the Japanese charged, and each time they were broken in blood. Eventually, Marine artillery and mortars joined the battle. In the end more than 800 of Ichiki's men were killed against the loss of 43 Marines killed and about 60 wounded.

General Hyakutake's counterstroke had failed, and Colonel Ichiki tasted the "fruits of victory" by burning his colors and shooting himself through the head.

The Battle of the Tenaru exhilarated the American Marines. For the first time they had met the Japanese in a pitched battle, and they had won a resounding victory. Although General Vandegrift was also pleased, he realized that one such battle did not make a campaign. The enemy's forces based on Rabaul still were far greater than his own on Guadalcanal. Moreover, the Japanese still controlled both the

sea and the sky. That meant that they could bring more troops to Guadalcanal to oust the Americans.

Up in Rabaul, this was exactly what General Hyakutake planned to do. At first, he had been astounded to hear of what had happened to Colonel Ichiki. He did not even know how to phrase his report to Tokyo. Annihilation simply had never happened to Japanese troops. So he reported: "The attack of the Ichiki Detachment was not entirely successful." Then, out of his new-found respect for the Americans, he ordered Major General Kiyotake Kawaguchi and his brigade of 5,000 Borneo veterans to take ship for Guadalcanal.

With this order, he gave to the Guadalcanal campaign its peculiar character. First, it was a battle for an island airfield. Next it was a race to reinforce and supply. Rarely before in history had there been a battle which so well expressed the axiom that whoever could "git thar fustest with the mostest" would be the winner. Perhaps never before had such a race been run on land, over the sea and through the air.

It continued day and night. By day, the Japanese flew down from Rabaul to bomb the Americans, while Vandegrift's handful of Marine pilots rose from Henderson Field to fight them off. Gradually this little "Cactus Air Force," assisted by Army and Navy pilots, wrested control of the skies from the enemy. Daylight also was the time when the Marines on the ground made their counterattacks, trying to expand their defensive circle or "perimeter." They also patrolled by day, seeking to learn of enemy movements in the dense jungle. Or else they strengthened their positions. Living off captured enemy rice, weakened by malaria and dysentery, plagued by clouds of mosquitoes and myriads of other sucking, stinging insects, drenched by monsoon rains or blistered by scorching tropical heat, the Marines still greeted the dawn of each day with a gay wisecrack or a glad sigh of relief.

That was because they dreaded the nights. It was at night that the Japanese attacked, swarming out of the jungle with shrieks and turkey-gobbler screeches of "Banzai! Banzai!" At night lone-wolf patrol planes—known as "Washing-Machine Charley" because of the sound of their motors— would circle for hours overhead, deliberately trying to keep the Marines awake. Then they would drop their bombs and fly away. If they dropped flares, however, then the nights would become even more hideous, because the flares were to mark targets for the big naval guns of the warships of the "Tokyo Express." Under the impact of huge shells weighing up to a ton, the very island seemed to buck and rear. Some nights the airfield would be ripped to pieces. Americans were blown to bits or buried in their pits or simply stunned by the dreadful roaring of enemy shells.

Because it was nighttime, the American aircraft were unable to rise to the attack. Thus Japanese destroyers, cruisers and even battleships could promenade Iron Bottom Bay at their leisure, battering the Marines for hours. Some hours before daylight, they headed home—racing to get out of range of the American aircraft which they knew would be rising at dawn. It was at night also that the Tokyo Express unloaded troops and supplies. Sometimes the American Navy tried to intercept the enemy ships, and when they did great naval battles were fought.

The first of these was called the Battle of the Eastern Solomons. In this air-sea fight, begun on August 24, the Americans sank the Japanese carrier *Ryujo* and turned back a major attempt to reinforce Guadalcanal. But the big American carrier *Enterprise* was knocked out of action for two months. Later the carrier *Saratoga* was knocked out of action for the rest of the Guadalcanal campaign. Then the Kawaguchi Brigade slipped through the American net. General Kawaguchi landed his men near the point where Colonel Ichiki had come ashore. They joined forces with the Ichiki survivors and the other Japanese on the island. Then they began marching toward the unprotected rear of Henderson Field.

The moment General Vandegrift learned of their landing, he ordered the Marine Raiders and paratroopers to move from Tulagi to Guadalcanal.

Colonel Merritt ("Red Mike") Ed-

Marines on dusk patrol crossing Lunga River.

son commanded the Raiders and paratroopers. Red Mike was a slender man, with blue eyes and a thatch of red hair. He was a born fighter and leader, and when he looked at a map of Guadalcanal his trained eyes at once saw the chink in the American armor.

"This looks like a good approach," he said in his throaty whisper, pointing to a ridge behind the airfield. It was a hogback which rose out of dense jungle before sloping gently down to Henderson Field. It was a natural highway into the heart of the Marine position. At once, General Vandegrift sent Edson and his men up to fortify the height that was to go into history as Bloody Ridge. At once, the enemy began bombing them from the sky and bombarding them from the sea. Obviously, Bloody Ridge was General Kawaguchi's objective. Almost as obvious, the Japanese were preparing for an all-out effort to retake Henderson Field.

From every quarter came reports of massing enemy ship and aircraft strength. Even Admiral Isoroku Yamamoto—Emperor Hirohito's "one and only Yamamoto," who had planned Pearl Harbor—was at sea at the head of the Japanese Combined Fleet. Admiral Turner flew in to Guadalcanal to inform General Vandegrift that his superiors at the American base in Noumea, on the island of New Caledonia, did not believe that Guadalcanal could be held. Vice-Admiral Robert L. Ghormley, Commander, South Pacific, had reported to Admiral

Beneath a camouflage net, Marines test a newly arrived pack howitzer.

Chester W. Nimitz in Hawaii that he could no longer support the Marines.

Another man might have been disheartened by such bad news. But Alexander Vandegrift's square jaw lifted.

Turning to his chief of staff, Colonel Gerald Thomas, the general said softly, "Jerry, we're going to defend this airfield until we no longer can. If that happens, we'll take what's left to the hills and fight guerrilla warfare." The Marines, he said, would never surrender.

On the afternoon of September 12, 42 Japanese aircraft bombed Edson's men on Bloody Ridge again. That night a Japanese cruiser and three destroyers slid into Iron Bottom Bay to shell them. Then a rocket rose from the jungle. Machine guns chattered, rifles barked—and Kawaguchi's men came rushing out of the jungle.

"Banzai!" they screamed. "Marine you die!"

As at the Tenaru, they sprinted into interlocking fire. Many fell, but they came on, and on the right flank they drove the Raiders back. But they could

128

not expand their penetration, and with daylight the Japanese melted into the jungle.

That day, to fool the enemy, Red Mike Edson pulled his men back 100 yards. This enabled him to shorten his lines and to force the enemy to go that much farther before closing with the Americans.

That night, the Japanese set off smoke bombs and cried out, "Gas attack!" in an effort to stampede the Marines. The trick did not work. Then 2,000 Japanese attacked chanting:

"U.S. Marines be dead tomorrow."

"U.S. Marines be dead tomorrow."

"You'll eat dirt first, you monkeys!" a Marine screamed, and the battle was on once more.

Once again the night sky above Bloody Ridge was slashed and crisscrossed with scarlet traces. It twinkled with muzzle blasts and it wailed with chattering steel and the hoarse cries of stricken and dying men. To this was added the baying of seven enemy destroyers firing on the Marine rear from Iron Bottom Bay, and the higher coughing of American artillery.

The Japanese seemed to be winning. The Americans were falling back. Scenting victory, the enemy pressed forward—and blundered into American artillery. Red Mike Edson had again shortened his position. Now he lay on his belly next to an artillery observer who was directing fire on the enemy.

"Closer," Edson whispered. "Closer."

It was too close. Marine shells fell even on Marine holes. But that dreadful rain broke the enemy charge.

Not all the Japanese fell, however. Three of them slipped through the Marine lines. With daybreak they had reached General Vandegrift's command post.

"Banzai!" they screamed. "Banzai!"

General Vandegrift looked up from messages he was reading outside his pavilion. He saw two Japanese soldiers and an officer who was swinging a huge two-handed saber. Hefting the saber like a spear, the officer hurled it at an American sergeant and transfixed him. Another sergeant rushed from a tent with a pistol and shot the enemy officer dead. Then a Marine corporal tried to shoot the soldiers, but his pistol jammed. He dove at them, just as almost everyone in the command post drew and fired—and the two men who menaced Vandegrift fell riddled.

Up on Bloody Ridge, the Marines were counterattacking—and the broken, dispirited remnant of the Kawaguchi Brigade had begun a long nightmarish retreat through the jungle.

The victory at Bloody Ridge was the critical point in the entire land campaign. But neither Vandegrift nor his Marines were aware of this. Instead, it seemed to them that they had merely postponed what appeared to be their doom. Moreover, two days after the attack ended, the big carriers *Wasp* and *Hornet* were steaming through the dangerous waters to the southeast which sailors called "Torpedo Junction." It was a cloudless blue day. Suddenly lookouts aboard *Wasp* cried out:

"Torpedoes!"

The warning came too late. Three enemy "fish" struck *Wasp* and whipsawed her like a piece of driftwood. In less than an hour the great ship was a floating funeral pyre, and she sank with a loss of 193 men. Now the Americans had only one aircraft carrier operational in the entire Pacific. The Japanese had four.

Then fortunes turned again. Admiral Turner risked the hidden wrath of Torpedo Junction to reinforce Vandegrift with another Marine regiment. Again a flip-flop: the Japanese countered as the Tokyo Express began to bring an entire enemy division to Guadalcanal. On the night of October 11, an American attempt to intercept the landing resulted in the Battle of Cape Esperance. It was a destroyer-cruiser slugging match, fought while the warriors of both nations huddled in their mudpits or jungle holes, and it was a stand-off. Nevertheless, the Japanese still seemed to hold the upper hand.

Night after night the Tokyo Express hammered at the Marines, and the gleaming black waters of Iron Bottom Bay clanged to the bellowing of "iron tongues of midnight." The bombardment rose to its horrible crescendo on October 13, what the Americans called the "Night of the Battleships." That night the Japanese battleships *Haruna* and *Kongo,* with a cruiser and seven destroyers, entered the Bay only a few hours after Admiral Turner had brought the first Army reinforcements to Guadalcanal. The soldiers of the 164th Infantry Regiment received a horrible baptism of fire.

Dawn of October 14 seemed like the night of American despair. Henderson Field was a wreck. Vandegrift's air force was all but destroyed. Dazed Marines, having stood firm under more than two months of punishment, were walking about like sleepwalkers. This was the low point of the campaign. And then, the very next day, American spirits soared again.

General Vandegrift received word that Admiral William ("Bull") Halsey had relieved Ghormley as South Pacific commander. Here was a true fighter of the Marines' own stamp. With their newly arrived Army comrades, the Marines knew Bull Halsey would not let them down. In proof of that faith, Admiral Halsey immediately summoned General Vandegrift to a dramatic high-level conference in Noumea.

All of the admiral's top advisers, including beetle-browed Richmond Kelly Turner, sat around a table to listen to Vandegrift's plea for more help. Smoking, silent, Bull Halsey heard him out.

Then Halsey asked, "Are we going to evacuate or hold?"

"I can hold," Alexander Vandegrift said softly. "But I've got to have more active support than I've been getting."

"All right," Bull Halsey said. "Go on back. I'll promise you everything I've got."

General Vandegrift did go back to Guadalcanal. But before he arrived there, the fiercest land-sea-air battle of the campaign had erupted.

Lieutenant General Haruyoshi Hyakutake had come to Guadalcanal to take personal command of the campaign. He had about 22,000 men, perhaps more than the Americans. He also had all of Rabaul's vast air power

at his disposal, as well as the striking power of Admiral Yamamoto's Combined Fleet.

Hyakutake planned a two-pronged attack on Henderson Field. The main blow was to fall behind the field, at roughly the same place where General Kawaguchi had failed. The other would come from the west against the Marines holding the Matanikau River line. In the meantime airplanes from Rabaul and the new bases in the Northern Solomons would bomb the Americans from the sky, while the Combined

Henderson Field. Pierced steel matting has been laid down to make temporary runways.

Fleet's gunfire ships scourged them from the sea. Once the airfield fell, planes from Yamamoto's carriers would fly in to take possession of it.

With this plan, Hyakutake set in motion the bellowing three-ring circus of death which the Americans called "Dugout Sunday." They called it that because a dugout was the most desirable place to be on that clanging, roaring, shattering 25th of October.

It began behind Henderson Field. Here Major General Masao Maruyama had marched with most of his famous Sendai Division. To Maruyama was to fall the honor of seizing the airfield. Unfortunately for him, his path was barred by a battalion of Marines under the celebrated Lieutenant Colonel Lewis B. ("Chesty") Puller. Chesty's nickname came from his enormous rib cage, puffing out like a pouter pigeon's. He also had a voice like a bullhorn, and his feats of bravery during Marine actions in the Caribbean had already made him a legend in the Corps. In Colonel Puller's command were tough young professionals of his own breed—men like Sergeant Manila John Basilone, who was in charge of a machine-gun section. At night, in a heavy rain, these men heard Sendai troops rushing at them screaming:

"Blood for the Emperor!"

"To hell with your Emperor!" a Marine yelled back. "Blood for Franklin and Eleanor!"

Even as the battle began, some Marines chuckled to hear this sardonic reference to President Roosevelt and his wife. But then there was no time for laughter. The Japanese were charging in massed thousands. The sodden ground shook. As the enemy reached the American barbed wire, the Marines opened up. Again and again, tan soldiers in mushroom helmets fell stricken. Others took their place. Still others flung themselves on the wire to form human bridges for their comrades. Over them came waves of Japanese, veering toward the center, now, straight toward the machine guns of Manila John Basilone.

Basilone's guns chattered and shook. His gunners fired them at full trigger. Enemy soldiers racing down an incline were tumbled in heaps. Still the guns sang. Steam hissed from their water jackets. Soon the red-hot barrels would have no cooling water. At once, the Marines urinated in the jackets—and the guns kept firing. Here was one of the critical points of the battle and here the Americans held. Because they did, Manila John Basilone was awarded the Medal of Honor.

Meanwhile, Chesty Puller was raging along the front lines, bellowing orders and encouragement to his men. When one of his company commanders used the field telephone to report that he was running out of ammunition, Puller snapped:

"You got bayonets, haven't you?"

"Sure. Yes, sir."

"All right, then. Hang on."

They did, everywhere. They still hung on the following night, when the

132

Marines push their way through the dense Guadalcanal jungle, keeping an eye out for Japanese snipers.

Sendai Division returned to the attack and when the 164th Infantry was fed into the battle. The American soldiers held firmly beside the veteran Marines. In the end, the Sendai Division was defeated and all but destroyed.

So, too, was General Hyakutake's western thrust repulsed. This tank-led attack had begun prematurely, and had been ended almost before it began when the Marines on the Matanikau knocked out the tanks. Then a second attempt to pierce the Marine lines was also hurled back during fighting which brought a Medal of Honor to a handsome Marine sergeant named Mitchell Paige. On the ground, then, the Japanese had failed.

In the air, the Americans blasted the enemy from the skies. On Dugout Sunday alone they shot down 26 airplanes, sank a cruiser and damaged a pair of destroyers.

At sea, the massive naval-air Battle of the Santa Cruz Islands started the day after Dugout Sunday. The battle began as *Enterprise,* now repaired, rushed up to join *Hornet* in an attempt to intercept the Combined Fleet and prevent Japanese bombardment of Guadalcanal. It ended in near disaster for the Americans. *Hornet* was lost and *Enterprise* was damaged once again. Even though this bold counter-stroke by Admiral Halsey had helped to save Guadalcanal, it left the Americans with only a single damaged carrier in the Pacific.

The Battle of the Santa Cruz Islands convinced the Japanese that they had gained the upper hand. Emperor Hirohito proudly told his nation: "The Combined Fleet is at present striking heavy blows at the enemy Fleet in the South Pacific Ocean. We are deeply gratified."

Well he might be. Only the crippled *Enterprise* stood between his forces and the battered Americans on Guadalcanal.

General Hyakutake and Admiral Yamamoto quickly took the initiative. Night after night the Tokyo Express brought more troops and guns down the Slot. Japanese artillery brought the Americans under daily shellfire, in addition to routine bombing and naval bombardment. By early November, Hyakutake had 30,000 men against Vandegrift's force of 23,000. Then he and Yamamoto made their final plan. A whole new division was to be brought south, while another division

Led by native guides, Marine Raiders move into the Guadalcanal hills.

and a brigade then in China were alerted for movement to Guadalcanal. When all was in readiness, a final knockout drive would be launched, supported from the air and the sea.

To counter this attack, Admiral Halsey had his own fleet—two battleships and eight cruisers, with supporting destroyers—a huge crew of craftsmen working night and day at Noumea to repair *Enterprise,* and a regiment each of Marines and soldiers. Halsey threw everything in to hold Guadalcanal. On November 11, Rear Admiral Norman Scott arrived at Guadalcanal with the Marine regiment. That same day *Enterprise* put to sea with repairmen still swarming over her decks and with her forward elevator still jammed. On November 12, Admiral Turner's ships entered Iron Bottom Bay with the Army regiment.

That afternoon, the Americans beat off a determined aerial attack. Late in the day, Admiral Turner received word that the enemy's big push was scheduled for that night. The big battleships *Hiei* and *Kirishima,* the cruiser *Nagara* and 14 destroyers were already sailing down the Slot. Mission: bombard Henderson Field. Once the field was wrecked, twelve Tokyo Express destroyers would arrive next day to put the 38th Division ashore on Guadalcanal. Meanwhile, other battleships and two carriers would be sailing 150 miles to the north in long-range support.

Admiral Turner could not allow Henderson Field to be shelled. He *had*

to prevent the arrival of Japanese troops. But with what? All he had was his own escort of cruisers and destroyers with which to stop battleships. Nevertheless, he sent them in. Turner ordered Rear Admiral Daniel Callaghan to attack the enemy bombardment force.

With his heavy cruisers *Atlanta, San Francisco* and *Portland,* his light cruisers *Helena* and *Juneau* and eight destroyers, Callaghan waited in Iron Bottom Bay for the mighty *Hiei* and *Kirishima* and their 15 smaller sisters. Unfortunately, the surprise that should have been his was squandered by poor communications. It was not until eight minutes after the foe was seen that "Uncle Dan" Callaghan shouted: "Commence firing! Give them hell, boys!"

Plunging straight ahead, the outgunned and outweighed Americans began what was perhaps the most furious sea fight ever fought. It was ship-for-ship, gun-for-gun, the great vessels maneuvering wildly over the narrow waters of the bay, their keels carving out glistening wakes on its opaque black surface. Ashore, the men of both nations crouched fearfully under the thunderclapping of the guns. Japanese and American, they sensed that the critical moment had arrived. They knew that they were helpless to control their fate, that the great campaign was being decided out there on the bay, where star shells rose with horrible red brilliance, where huge red tracers streaked across the black sky like strings of lighted boxcars over a hill.

Out there, Admiral Callaghan was crying: "We want the big ones, boys, we want the big ones!"

Out there, three little American destroyers did go after big *Hiei*. The guns of the great Japanese battleship spouted flame and smoke and two of the little Yanks were sunk. Then Callaghan's own flag cruiser *San Francisco* took on *Hiei*. Again the battleship fired. Shells tore into the American bridge, killing Admiral Callaghan. More enemy shells sank *Atlanta* and *Juneau* and two more destroyers and killed another admiral, Norman Scott. The Americans suffered grievously. Only one of the 13 U.S. ships escaped enemy gunfire.

Yet they had sunk two enemy destroyers and so crippled great *Hiei* that she could be sunk by American aircraft during daylight. More important, the American ships forced the other enemy ships to retire. Henderson Field had been saved.

But not for long. That very night another Japanese force of six cruisers and six destroyers came down the Slot. An American battleship force under Rear Admiral Willis ("Ching") Lee was too far away to intercept it. So was the carrier *Enterprise*. Henderson Field was bombarded that night. But not with the accuracy or the weight that might have been possible with battleships. Even though Admiral Gunichi Mikawa triumphantly announced destruction of the American air base, with daylight American

pilots sprinted for their armed planes to roar aloft after Mikawa's ships.

The American pilots found the Japanese ships. They put a pair of torpedoes into the cruiser *Kinugasa,* leaving her a sitting duck for pilots from *Enterprise,* and they damaged three other cruisers. More important—most important—they found the Tokyo Express. Eleven transports stuffed with Japanese soldiers were spotted sailing over a calm sea, and now the hideous slaughter known as the "Buzzard Patrol" was begun.

Flying in from everywhere—from Henderson, from *Enterprise,* from faraway Espiritu Santo and the Fijis —American aircraft of every type bombed and strafed the helpless enemy. Six Japanese transports were sunk and a seventh sent limping home. The waters of the Slot were reddened. When the remaining four Japanese transports did reach Guadalcanal they had to be beached.

Now it was night again, the darkness of November 14. Now Admiral Ching Lee entered Iron Bottom Bay with the battleships *Washington* and *South Dakota* and four destroyers. He was looking for a third Japanese bombardment force: the mighty battleship *Kirishima* escorted by four cruisers and nine destroyers.

One again, the Japanese drew first blood. They fired shoals of torpedoes, mortally wounding three American destroyers. Then *Kirishima* caught *South Dakota* in her searchlights and began battering her. The Americans

General Vandegrift (left), revisiting Guadalcanal a year after his bitter struggle there.

fought back, shooting out the search-lights—and then *Washington* found *Kirishima*. Again and again her great 16-inch guns hurled huge shells into the enemy. Soon *Kirishima* joined *Hiei* on the bottom of the sea, together with two of her escorting destroyers.

And that was the end of the three-day Naval Battle of Guadalcanal.

The three-month struggle for the control of Guadalcanal had turned the tide of victory. After it was over, the Americans controlled the sea and the sky. They could reinforce and supply Guadalcanal at will, while preventing the enemy from doing the same. In December command on Guadalcanal passed from Alexander Vandegrift of the Marines to Alexander Patch of the Army. And the 1st Marine Division, which had borne the brunt of what a British observer called "a feat of arms which remains unsurpassed," was finally relieved.

Waiting until he had enough men to outnumber the enemy, General Patch went over to the attack. With a force now more Army than Marine, he sought to crush Hyakutake's riddled remnant. Now the Imperial General Headquarters in Tokyo became divided over whether to reinforce or evacuate Guadalcanal. There were bitter arguments. Blows were struck. At last, it was decided to evacuate. In early February, 1943, the Tokyo Express made its final run down the Slot to draw off Hyakutake and his men.

So the tide turned on Guadalcanal. When it did, so also turned the tide of war in the Pacific. Up until Guadalcanal, the Japanese victory flood had been irresistible. It had been checked at Midway, but even after that great battle the Japanese were still on the offensive. After Guadalcanal, however —after the combined services of both nations confronted each other in pitched battle—the Japanese were forever on the defensive.

"After Coral Sea and Midway, I still had hope," said one high-ranking Japanese naval officer. "But after Guadalcanal I felt that we could not win."

And they did not.

NORMANDY
Eisenhower's Great Gamble

In the early-morning blackness of June 5, 1944, a near-hurricane wind howled around Portsmouth on the coast of southern England. Rain poured from the skies, sometimes being seized by the wind and flung in horizontal sheets.

This was the fateful storm that had begun to rage the previous day. This was the wind and the rain that had turned the English Channel into an angry, choppy gray sea and heaped the surf high on the coast of northern France. Because of this wind and rain, General Dwight D. Eisenhower had been compelled to postpone the great Allied invasion of France scheduled for June 5.

It had been a difficult decision for the general. Only a few days in June would be suitable for a landing. The tides had to be right for the boats to get ashore, and there had to be a moon shining for paratroopers to make a

138

night jump. June 5 had seemed to fulfill these conditions best. Now the general could only hope that the storm would subside before the few remaining "good days" were used up.

But the storm wailed on in all its fury, hurling its sheets of rain against the buildings and tents in General Eisenhower's little camp at Portsmouth. It continued as the general and his staff took the bumpy mile-long ride to the naval headquarters, where they were to receive another briefing on the weather.

General Eisenhower's face was grim as he went inside and sat on a sofa. He listened intently as Group Captain J. M. Stagg, the chief weatherman, told him that the storm had been so fierce on the French coast that the Allied invasion would surely have met disaster. Then Captain Stagg spoke directly to the Supreme Commander.

"I think we have found a gleam of hope for you, sir. The mass of weather fronts coming in from the Atlantic is moving faster than we anticipated. We predict there will be rather fair conditions beginning late on June 5 and lasting until the next morning, June 6, with a drop in wind velocity and some break in the clouds."

Here was an unexpected pause in the storm. Should General Eisenhower risk it? If not, he might have to accept a month's delay. Hitler, as he knew, had failed in Russia because of just such a loss of time. Hitler's army, reaching Moscow in December instead of November, had been trapped in an early Russian winter. A month lost to the Allies could also mean a disastrous late start for the advance into Germany itself.

For fully five minutes, the Supreme Commander sat in silence on the sofa. His face was tense and grave. Suddenly, he looked up. His face was calm.

"Okay," he said briskly. "We'll go."

D-Day, as the first day of an invasion is called, was to be one of the most momentous single days in the history of Europe and America. Both sides looked upon it as an all-or-nothing battle. If the Allies succeeded, France would rise again, and the dusk of the Third Reich would fall upon Adolf Hitler and his henchmen. If the Allies failed, then hope of freedom would die in France, and the heel of the Nazi jackboot would press down harder upon a prostrate Europe.

Even though Hitler had begun to taste defeat, he was still confident that his forces could hold *Festung Europa* —his "Fortress Europe." He still believed in his destiny, always forgetting his latest setback by remembering his earlier glories.

Austria, Czechoslovakia, Rumania, Hungary and Bulgaria, these five nations had fallen to his "diplomacy" backed up by naked force. His *Wehrmacht* or war machine had conquered Poland, Norway, Denmark, Luxembourg, Holland, Belgium, France, North Africa, Yugoslavia, Greece and Crete. Great Russia had been invaded, and mighty Britain driven from the Continent to watch in despair while the Axis knife cut deeper through her Mediterranean lifeline to her far-flung empire.

In less than two years—by the summer of 1941—the high civilization of Europe lay helpless at Hitler's feet. How had it all happened so fast?

The answer was that the Germans under Hitler had worked warfare's fourth revolution. The first one, the Democratic Revolution, had made all citizens liable to service. The second, the Industrial, had equipped these huge armies with horribly efficient new weapons. The third, the Managerial, had led commanders to conduct the business of war with the same impersonal efficiency as the manager of a business enterprise. Now the fourth, the Mechanical, had harnessed these weapons to the internal-combustion engine. Tanks and airplanes armed with the latest machine guns, cannon and bombs now made it possible to fight Hitler's own brand of "lightning war" known as the *blitzkrieg*.

Between them, Hitler's swift-moving armor and aircraft struck at an enemy army's "brains." These are his headquarters behind the lines which control the army's "body"—its troops. The blitzkrieg also paralyzed the army's "nerve centers"—the communications systems over which reports and orders are transmitted and the highways over which troops must move.

From the skies, German aircraft bombed railroads, highways, bridges, airfields and radio stations. They raided cities and drove terrified residents out on the roads, thus making military movement even more difficult. On the ground, the tanks burst through lightly armed infantry to swoop down on headquarters sections. They took highways and seized vital crossroads. In this way, their victim's brains and nerve centers were knocked out and the great demoralized "body" of his army was left leaderless and helpless.

That was the blitzkrieg which did so much for Hitler. But then he invaded Russia. Swiftly as his panzer or armored divisions might move, far as his aircraft might fly, the vast Russian spaces were simply too much to be so suddenly conquered. Russian roads were poor. Tanks had trouble moving over them. The Russian countryside had been "scorched"—deliberately burned by the inhabitants—leaving nothing for the invaders. Then, in December, the cruel white Russian winter froze Hitler's advancing armies in its grasp and all chance of conquering Russia disappeared.

This, of course, was not realized at the time. Hitler still believed himself invincible. However, in that same December of 1941, Japan made the enormous error of attacking Pearl Harbor. That brought the United States into the war against Hitler. It put all of America's matchless industrial capacity at the disposal of the Allies. Eventually tanks, airplanes and weapons of all descriptions poured out of the American arsenal in a flood of steel. By then the Allies, too, had adopted the tactics of the blitzkrieg.

In North Africa, a British general named Bernard Montgomery began a counterattack. His tanks and airplanes seized the initiative. They drove back the Italians and Germans under General Erwin Rommel, the famous leader whose victories had earned him the nickname of the "Desert Fox." In November of 1942, the Allies invaded North Africa. British and American divisions under General Eisenhower made a series of landings in an effort to trap Rommel. Although Eisenhower and Montgomery could not catch Rommel, they did succeed in capturing most of his army.

This was Hitler's first defeat. Another followed quickly at the big island of Sicily off the coast of Italy. This freed the Mediterranean from Axis control. Next, Italy was invaded. Mussolini fell from power. Still, Hitler remained unshaken. He was certain that he could stop the Allies in Italy, positive he could keep them out of France.

But then Dwight D. Eisenhower, the general who had given the Germans their first setbacks, was called to London to be Supreme Commander of the cross-Channel invasion.

Known as "Ike" to both premiers and privates, this warm, friendly commander with the broad grin and bright blue eyes was probably the most popular general in American history. "I like Ike," was a common saying, not only

General Erwin Rommel

among the troops or the folks back home, but also among the Allied commanders.

This attractiveness in Eisenhower was an important quality in a man leading an armed coalition. Coalition warfare, in which several nations fight together against a common foe, is the most difficult of all. There are so many differences—in language, dress, habits, weapons, military "doctrine"—that they often prove divisive. Worst of all is national pride, which always seems to be wounded when some "foreigner" is given an important command.

Dwight Eisenhower was well aware

of this. He knew that even the campaigns of the great Napoleon were made easier by the fact that he was always leading a unified French army against a divided coalition. Ike had no intention of allowing his own army of Americans, British, French, Canadians, Belgians, Poles and others to become torn by dissension. One of his first moves was to bring General Montgomery to London and place him in command of all ground forces. This mollifiied the peppery Montgomery, as well as other British generals who resented seeing a "Yank" named Supreme Commander.

In truth, the Americans deserved the top post, because they were supplying by far the greatest number of troops and largest volume of equipment. Within six months, no less than 1,627,000 American soldiers and 53,000 sailors had assembled in southern England. Embarkation ports as far away as Wales were thronged with ships, and their wharves were piled high with boxes and crates and every manner of vehicle or gun.

Not all of these men and arms were to cross the English Channel to France on the first day. Nevertheless, the crossing was to be the largest amphibious invasion in all history. No less than 5,300 ships and craft were to carry 107,000 men, 14,000 vehicles and 14,500 tons of supplies across the wind-swept Channel on that momentous D-Day. Another 43,000 airborne troops were to be flown into battle by part of the 12,000 aircraft—the mightiest aerial armada ever assembled—which would also support the invasion. Even before D-Day the Anglo-American aircraft would be thundering over France and Germany to blast the enemy's beach defenses, knock out his bridges and railroads and shoot up his rear areas. When D-Day did come, the big guns of a massive Anglo-American bombardment fleet would batter the enemy's coastal positions.

In effect, General Eisenhower was sailing the equivalent of a big modern city to war. Almost everything required to run such a city would be transported to France. This included telephone exchanges, power plants, radio stations, laundries, bakeries, hospitals, prisons and police stations, buses and railroad locomotives, to say nothing of huge volumes of ammunition, food, clothing, fuel and medical supplies, together with fleets of tanks and trucks and every conceivable type of military vehicle—and a freshly printed supply of French money.

Because the huge Allied host was landing across open beaches, there were even portable ports called Mulberries. These were enormous concrete structures resembling six-story buildings lying on their sides. Two of them were built to be towed across the Channel and sunk off the invasion beaches. There, they would serve as sheltered docks able to receive ships in any kind of weather. There were also Gooseberries—groups of old ships to be sunk in a stem-to-stern line to form a breakwater. To keep the battlefront supplied with a steady flow of fuel—the lifeblood of modern war—special flexible undersea pipelines were to be laid across the Channel.

Thus, the preparations, so vast and various, were eloquent testimony to the arrival of the fifth revolution in warfare—the Scientific Revolution. For all of these gadgets and devices, as well as those developed by the Germans to defend their Fortress Europe, had been produced by what may be called the "battle of the drawing boards." This was the struggle between rival scientists—designers, researchers and engineers—to provide their armies with superior weapons. Napoleon had once said, "God is on the side of the big battalions." But now that cynical remark could be altered to read, "God is on the side of the latest models." And it would be true. Rare indeed was the World War II campaign that ended with exactly the same weapons with which it had been begun. Communications being so rapid, information could at once be relayed from the battlefield to the weapons laboratory, where a scientist could either immediately correct a defect in his own new weapons or exploit a flaw in the enemy's.

In preparation for D-Day, Eisenhower added a final touch of deception. Guessing that his opponent, Field Marshal Gerd von Rundstedt, expected him to cross over the short Dover-to-Calais route, Ike chose to take the longer crossing to Normandy instead. This was because Normandy was less strongly defended. Of the 50 German divisions in France, only eight were in the vicinity of the 60-mile strip of Normandy beach which Ike had chosen. But there were 19 German divisions in the Calais area.

Hoping to keep them there, Ike built an elaborate dummy "headquarters" in Dover. Divisions not to be used on D-Day were quartered there. Details of the "Calais invasion" were deliberately leaked to known enemy agents. Calais and its surroundings were bombed almost as heavily as Normandy.

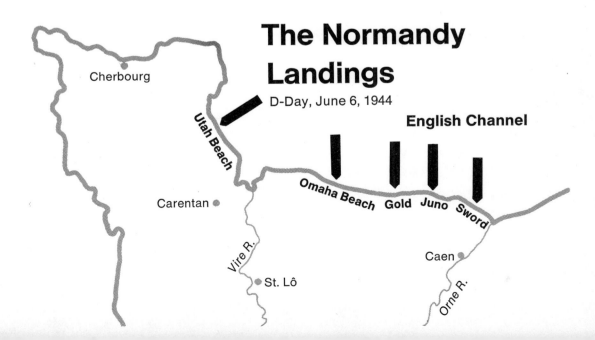

The Normandy Landings

D-Day, June 6, 1944

English Channel

Cherbourg

Utah Beach

Omaha Beach Gold Juno Sword

Carentan

Vire R.

St. Lô

Caen

Orne R.

View of the French coast at low tide, showing the mines and other booby traps that Rommel planted to stop Allied landing craft.

The trick worked. Marshal von Rundstedt held the bulk of his forces in the Calais area.

Unfortunately for Eisenhower and his soldiers, however, the man in charge of defending Normandy was General Rommel—the Desert Fox.

Erwin Rommel had been working for months on the defenses of the Atlantic Wall. An army of soldiers and laborers had been busy pouring concrete, putting most of Rommel's guns under bombproof roofs. They mined the beach exits. Offshore they sowed the sand with millions of mines, "dragon's teeth" and hedgehogs. Out in the open fields they planted *Rommelspargel* ("Rommel's asparagus")— tall, mined poles which would prevent glider or paratroop landings. With the approach of June, 1944, the Normandy beaches bristled with guns and obstacles.

Meanwhile, Rommel began moving his troops forward. In this, he disagreed with his chief, Marshal von Rundstedt. Rundstedt believed that he should allow the Allies to land and then hit them with his massed reserves. Rommel, remembering Africa, realized that Allied air power would make it impossible to move up the reserves. He insisted that Fortress Europe must be defended at the water's edge. The titanic battle would be won on the beaches or not at all. Rundstedt, however, was not persuaded. Because of this, Rommel did not have all his armor in a forward position. Nevertheless, he continued to prepare his forces for an all-or-nothing struggle on the beaches.

"The first twenty-four hours will be decisive," he said. "The fate of Germany depends on the outcome. For Germany, it will be the longest day."

But then came the storm of June 4. When it howled on through June 5, Rommel decided that the Allies would never risk landing in such weather. So he went back to Germany to be with his wife on her birthday.

Not long after General Eisenhower

decided to risk the weather, he sat down to write a communiqué. It read:

OUR LANDINGS IN THE CHERBOURG-HAVRE AREA HAVE FAILED TO GAIN A SATISFACTORY FOOTHOLD AND I HAVE WITHDRAWN THE TROOPS. MY DECISION TO ATTACK AT THIS TIME AND PLACE WAS BASED UPON THE BEST INFORMATION AVAILABLE. THE TROOPS, THE AIR, AND THE NAVY, DID ALL THAT BRAVERY AND DEVOTION TO DUTY COULD DO. IF ANY BLAME OR FAULT ATTACHES TO THE ATTEMPT IT IS MINE ALONE.

Signing his name with the fervent hope that he would never have to issue that communiqué, Dwight D. Eisenhower put the slip of paper in a pocket of his battle jacket. Then, to his great joy, he saw that the gloom of June 5 was giving way. The day was ending in a burst of sunshine. The air of the long English summer twilight was golden. Shorn of his greatest fear, Ike drove out to the camp of the 101st Airborne Division.

The paratroopers were a cocky group. Some had shaved their heads to leave only an Indian scalp lock. Others had daubed coal black beneath their eyes or put on Indian war paint. Their helmets were camouflaged. In their pockets were ten dollars' worth of that newly printed French money. They also carried inexpensive metal crickets to signal each other in the dark. One squeeze *(click-clack)* would be answered by two *(click-clack, click-clack)*.

The paratroopers joked with Ike.

They told him not to worry. Little did they realize how much Ike worried about them. That was because so much depended on the airborne troops.

On the left of the Normandy invasion area, where the British and Canadians were to land, the terrain was fairly simple. But on the right, behind the beaches called "Omaha" and "Utah" by the Americans, was a wide lagoon. Causeways ran through this lagoon. If the Germans held those causeways, they could keep the Americans from getting inland. Unit after American unit would pile up, one upon another. They would become crowded into a tiny space which Rommel's gunners could then turn into a slaughter pen.

To prevent this, General Eisenhower decided to drop two divisions of American airborne troops behind the beaches. They were to seize the lagoon causeways, and thus open exits from

General Eisenhower talking to paratroopers a few hours before their drop into Normandy. The men have blackened their faces for camouflage in night fighting.

the beaches. It was a dangerous assignment, so fraught with peril that Eisenhower's own air commander, Air Chief Marshal Sir Trafford Leigh-Mallory, opposed it at the last minute. Leigh-Mallory argued against what he called the "futile slaughter" of two splendid divisions. He believed that they would become bogged down in swampy ground and gobbled up piecemeal by the Germans. This protest, coming on the eve of the invasion, compelled General Eisenhower to make an anguished, last-minute review of his plans. In the end, he decided that the night jump was vital to the invasion. But even as he spoke words of encouragement to the splendid young Americans who were to jump into enemy-held France that night, there was sorrow in his heart. He realized that many of them would not see the sunlight of June 6.

Night began to fall.

From the Irish Sea to the Channel the great dark shapes of the invasion fleet sortied. Eastward they sailed. Watchers on the headlands of southern England could see them coming for mile after mile. Behind them the western sun was dying. Its pale light outlined the great masts of battleships. It fell upon squat tugboats and landing ships that looked like seagoing bathtubs. A red halo seemed to encircle the great barrage balloons being towed to the battle by sleek, graceful destroyers.

Now, overhead, came the murmuring of many motors. Wave after wave of aircraft mounted the night sky and set their course for France. Throughout the night it continued, this massive throbbing, this coming and going of the skycraft, this mingling roar of their engines.

Now the airborne transports were over Normandy. Enemy antiaircraft fire reached for them. Up came the tracers like long red streaks of confetti. The night sky flashed and popped with shell bursts. The American planes began to "bounce and bob like a ball on a waterspout." Now they were over the drop zones. Now the jumpmasters were crouched at the open, whistling doorways.

"Stand up!"

"Hook on!"

"Check equipment!"

The green lights came on, and out into empty blackness leaped the yelling paratroopers. Lighted by moonlight, or wrapped in billowing mists, the Americans came down to France. Some fell in the sea and drowned because their planes were off course. Others fell in the swamps. Weighted by weapons, caught in their harness, some drowned in three feet of water. Most of them were scattered. Some paratroopers landed 25 miles from their objective. Others, landing on hard ground, broke their legs in the fall.

Lieutenant Colonel Benjamin Vandervoort broke his ankle, but he fought through the entire campaign on a stirrup-crutch rigged for him by his medics. Major General Matthew B.

Ridgway, commander of the 82nd Airborne Division, came down in a soft, grassy field. He spilled the air from his chute and unbuckled his harness, only to lose his .45-caliber pistol in the darkness. Suddenly, he heard movement. He tensed. There, outlined in the dim moonlight, was a large, friendly cow. For a moment General Ridgway felt like kissing her. But then he began to rally his division.

It was a difficult task because the Americans were scattered far and wide. Yet that very dispersion confused the enemy. They were not sure of the American objective. They did not know where to defend, nor could they concentrate their own forces. Thus, the battle behind the beaches became man against man, squad against squad. Men struggled and died in hedgerows and swamps, in open fields and through the streets of sleepy little towns—hamlets that were now sleepless and terrified amid the general wail of combat. Overhead, meanwhile, flew the thousand-plane Allied bombing fleets. Antiaircraft fire trailed its long red streamers towards them. Sometimes there were hits, and the great four-engine craft exploded and plummeted like falling stars. Everywhere was the hideous crash of falling bombs and the rumble of reverberating earth.

Gradually, now, the Americans gathered their forces. They seized and held the vital causeways. Now, it was up to the landing troops to seize the beaches.

Daylight off Normandy broke with a roar of guns. The noise was constant, incredible. Mighty battleships promenaded the Channel to hurl their huge shells at the German positions. Little destroyers ran boldly inshore to rake the beaches. Rocket ships fired, and there was a monstrous swooshing as the missiles rose in visible flights to go arching toward the enemy. Always, overhead, there was the constant rumble of aircraft motors, and on the beaches the crashing of bombs.

Inside their positions, the German soldiers gaped at the enormous Allied fleet. Stretching for 60 miles along the coast of Normandy was a line of landing craft trailing their white wakes as they raced for the beaches. Allied minesweepers cleared the offshore water. Some hit mines and blew up with a roar. Coming in closer, frogmen in green rubber suits leaped daringly into the sea to blow up underwater obstacles and clear a path for the landing boats.

In they came. The naval and aerial bombardment lifted, and the stunned Germans shook themselves and began firing back. Everywhere, the assault boats took hits. Everywhere the famous DD (dual-drive) tanks that had been rigged to "swim" ashore were sinking in the heavy sea. On the left flank, the British and Canadians landed on the beaches called Sword, Juno and Gold. On the right, the first Americans to land were those hitting Utah Beach on the far right.

Yelling like Indians, the spearhead

One small part of the vast Allied fleet en route to Normandy.

troops of the 4th Infantry Division leaped from their boats into waist-deep water. "We're on French soil!" they shouted, brandishing their rifles. Luckily for them, they had been landed at the wrong place—on a lightly defended beach. Soon they were moving inland.

Into Utah also came a company of Rangers. Hand-picked and rigorously trained, they had the dangerous mission of seizing a 100-foot cliff where enemy artillery was believed to be emplaced. Coming ashore, 15 of the Rangers were hit. But the survivors set up mortars and fired ropes and rope ladders fitted with grapnel hooks at the cliff. Some of the hooks caught, and the Rangers began climbing.

The Germans shot down the leading men. They cut the ropes. Out at sea, an American destroyer came to the rescue, sweeping inshore to take the enemy under fire. Hand over hand, the Rangers kept climbing. They reached the top—and found it empty. The Germans had fled, and the guns that menaced Omaha Beach farther left had been moved inland.

But if enemy artillery did not defend Omaha, there was something there far worse: a crack enemy division. Brought to the bluffs above Omaha for practice maneuvers, the 352nd Division now poured a terribly real and killing fire into the invading Americans.

Of the six boats carrying the 116th

Assault troops struggle ashore at Omaha Beach on D-Day. In the background, shrouded by gunsmoke, looms the cliff from which German machine guns pour a deadly fire onto the beach.

Infantry Regiment's spearhead troops, one sank, another was stopped by shell-fire and the other four were halted at a sand bar. When the landing ramps came down, the soldiers jumped into water that was from waist-high to shoulder-high. And then, in the words of the unit report:

"As if this were the signal for which the enemy had waited, all boats came under criss-cross machine-gun fire. . . . As the first men jumped, they crumpled and flopped into the water. Then order was lost. It seemed to the men that the only way to get ashore was to dive head first in and swim clear of the fire that was striking the boats. But, as they hit the water, their heavy equipment dragged them down and soon they were struggling to keep afloat. Some were hit in the water and wounded. Some drowned then and there. . . .

"But some moved safely through the bullet-fire to the sand and then, finding they could not hold there, went back into the water and used it as cover, only their heads sticking out. Those who survived kept moving forward with the tide, sheltering at times behind under-water obstacles, and in this way they finally made their landings.

"Within ten minutes of the ramps being lowered, A Company had become inert, leaderless and almost incapable of action. Every officer and sergeant had been killed or wounded. . . . It had become a struggle for survival and rescue. The men in the water pushed wounded men ashore ahead of them, and those who had reached the sands crawled back into the water pulling others to land to save them from drowning, in many cases only to see the rescued men wounded again or to be hit themselves. Within 20 minutes of striking the beach A Company had ceased to be an assault company and had become a forlorn little rescue party bent upon survival and the saving of lives."

A thick eddying cloud of smoke now hung over the 60-mile battlefront. At both ends of that line—with the British-Canadians on the left and the Americans at Utah on the far right— the fight was going well. But at Omaha in the right center, it was not. At Omaha boatload after boatload of terrified soldiers was piling up on the beach. Again and again units of the 1st and 29th Divisions were landed at the wrong place. Or they were just dumped into the water by coxswains who wanted only to flee that hideous place where death blossomed in shell bursts or whistled hidden over the surf and the sands. Groups of soldiers huddled in horror among the dead and the dying, sometimes trying to take cover behind the growing number of wrecked vehicles.

Omaha's surfline and offshore waters were clogged with debris. Everywhere were life jackets, wrecked boats, sunken tanks, mattresses, all manner of supplies—and bodies. As the water heaved, so did the line of debris. Now boats coming into the battle passed men in life jackets, men paddling on life rafts. These were the survivors of the sunken DD tanks or of the gun lighters that never got the precious artillery ashore in time.

Sometimes the coxswains found boat channels blasted through the enemy underwater obstacles by Navy underwater demolition teams. Oftentimes the UDT men stood on each other's shoulders to defuze enemy mines. But there were too many mines, and too often luckless American boats blundered into them and blew up.

Omaha had become the critical point in the entire Allied line. If the Germans could hurl the Americans into the sea at Omaha, they would cut the Allied line in two. They would be free to isolate the other American force at Utah and then to pin the British-Canadian beachhead against the sea.

Still, the Americans were ashore on Omaha. Even though the Germans on the bluffs above them continued to fire down their throats, even though many of the Americans lay paralyzed with fear, they were there. Now, two hours after the first touch-down, the problem was to get the men off the beach. They had to drive inland. To get into the German positions and silence them, the Americans would have to cross 50 to 300 yards of sand.

"Come on!" yelled gallant young officers and NCOs to their men. "Let's get the hell off this beach!" Sometimes they taunted their men, crying, "Let's see what you're made of!" Or, "Get your yellow behind up there!"

152

Foreground: GIs rest briefly in the comparative safety of a seawall. Background: others press inland over the crest of the dune.

When Colonel George Taylor came ashore, he found the men around him hugging an embankment and being riddled where they lay. He stood erect among them and yelled, "Two kinds of people are staying on this beach—the dead and those who are going to die! Now, let's get the hell out of here!"

It was so true. To lie on that awful beach, out of fear or a false sense of security, was merely to await death. Better to be up and charging the enemy, braving his fire to close with him and destroy him in his positions. Then and then only would Omaha be safe for the following troops to come in and punch even deeper inland through the first spearheads. That was

what the American officers on the beach were trying to do. Gradually they brought order out of chaos. Under the command of sergeants and junior officers—occasionally a resourceful, beardless private—the Americans began to rally. Then they began to join forces.

At noon the Anglo-American fleet bombarded the bluffs again. Destroyers and other small-fire ships ran in so close that they risked running aground, while the heavyweights stood offshore to hurl huge projectiles into the enemy positions. Throughout that long, bloody afternoon, the Americans built their attack. Slowly, inexorably, they punched toward the bluffs. At

By late afternoon of D-Day the beaches have been secured, and advance troops are pushing into the interior of Normandy.

three o'clock in the afternoon, a message went out to Lieutenant General Omar Bradley, commander of the American forces:

"Troops formerly pinned down on beaches [are] advancing up the heights behind the beaches."

Omaha was falling. It was falling to raw courage, to the bravery of men advancing into enemy fire protected only by their shirts. Nevertheless, the Germans did not quit. The advancing Americans still had to contend with barbed wire, bullets and exploding shells. Mines were everywhere to blow the unwary to bits. Yet by four o'clock the invaders had passed over the crest of the enemy hills and were punching toward the little inland towns. To their left, the British-Canadian forces still drove forward, making penetrations as deep as seven miles. To their right, the

Rangers and soldiers of the 4th Division had Utah safely in hand.

That was the situation report received by General Eisenhower aboard a destroyer bound from Portsmouth for the battlefield. Now the communiqué of defeat lying like lead in his pocket would not be needed. Instead, a jubilant Allied world heard that the landings were "proceeding according to plan."

Ike had gambled—and won. He had so completely deceived Marshal von Rundstedt that the German divisions concentrated around Calais could not get to Normandy in time. He had landed where he was least expected, and at a time when General Rommel believed he would not land at all.

Germany's "longest day" had been just long enough for the Allies to come back to France.

PUSAN-INCHON
MacArthur
Parries and Thrusts

After World War II ended, General of the Army Douglas MacArthur became Supreme Commander of American forces occupying Japan. He went to Tokyo to direct the rebuilding of a ruined nation, doing it so well that Japan became a bulwark of democracy in the Far East.

With this great feat, it would seem that Douglas MacArthur had crowned the most remarkable military career in American history. That career stretched back half a century, covering nearly half of America's wars. As a handsome young cadet at West Point, MacArthur stood at the top of his class with a scholastic record that remains unsurpassed. As a "shavetail" —a second lieutenant—in the Philippines, he had his hat knocked from his head by a rebel's bullet. During an incident in Mexico, MacArthur very nearly won a Medal of Honor. In World War I the dashing Douglas Mac-

155

Arthur was the youngest general in the American Expeditionary Forces, thereafter becoming the youngest superintendent at West Point, the youngest Chief of Staff (head of the Army) and the first Chief of Staff to serve two terms in peacetime.

That would seem enough for any soldier. Yet, after going on inactive status in 1935, MacArthur went to the Philippines to organize and command the new Philippine Army. Just before World War II he was recalled to active duty, and he was in the Philippines when Japan attacked Pearl Harbor. General MacArthur's dramatic escape from the Philippines was among the most stirring events of World War II. Yet it was surpassed by the brilliant island-hopping campaign which brought the general and his Americans back to Manila. After this, MacArthur received the Japanese surrender aboard the battleship *Missouri* and became chief of the Japanese occupation.

Now, it seemed, the old war-horse was out of harness for good. Figuratively he had hung up his sword. Actually he put away the old corncob pipe which he always smoked when visiting the front.

But then, on the Sunday morning of June 25, 1950, the telephone rang in MacArthur's bedroom in Tokyo. The caller spoke quickly, in an excited voice:

"General, we have just received a dispatch from Seoul! The North Koreans struck in great strength south across the 38th Parallel at four o'clock this morning!"

MacArthur was stunned. Only nine years earlier, at the same hour on another Sunday morning, another urgent caller had awakened him in Manila with the report of Pearl Harbor. Not again, the general thought; not again!

But it was true. South Korea had been invaded. The Communist North Koreans were even then streaming south, hoping to crush democracy in Korea before anyone could stop them. How had it happened, MacArthur asked himself in dismay; how had it happened?

War had come in Korea chiefly because President Roosevelt and Prime Minister Churchill thought they could get along with Premier Stalin of Russia after World War II. As a wartime ally, Russia had helped to crush Hitler. The Americans and the British hoped that the Russians would now help to build a free and peaceful postwar world. But Stalin had no such intentions.

Although he publicly proclaimed his desire that Japanese-held Korea should be free and independent, he secretly trained the agents who would make Korea a Communist puppet state dependent on Moscow. The leader of this band was a pudgy guerrilla fighter who called himself Kim Il Sung, after a famous Korean patriot.

After Japan surrendered, Stalin and Kim Il Sung saw their chance. For convenience, it had been agreed that the Americans would disarm Japanese troops in southern Korea and the Russians would disarm those in the north. The dividing line was placed at the 38th Parallel of north latitude, which cuts the 600-mile-long peninsula roughly in half.

The Americans certainly did not intend that this imaginary line should become a boundary dividing unhappy Korea into two zones. But the Russians did. So did Kim Il Sung and his fellow agents. Between them, they turned the 38th Parallel into an armed border. Then Kim was set up as a ruler in the city of Pyongyang.

Alarmed, the United States took the Korean problem to the United Nations. The General Assembly voted to hold free elections throughout the peninsula. Kim, however, refused to allow the UN commissioners north of the 38th Parallel. Nevertheless, an election was held south of it. Syngman Rhee, an aged patriot, was elected the first president of the Republic of Korea with a capital at Seoul. Soon the new nation came to be called South Korea.

In reply, Kim Il Sung held rigged elections which established himself as premier of the Communist state of North Korea. Neither Kim nor Stalin was satisfied with this situation, however. Both wanted to put all of Korea in the Communist camp.

Thus, with vast Russian assistance, Kim built a modern army. In South Korea, the American-backed Rhee government also organized an army. But it was not nearly as strong as North Korea's. Then, in 1949, the Communists won control of China. This made North Korea bolder, because her enormous neighbor was now a Communist nation like herself. Finally, when top American officials began making statements suggesting that the United States would not fight to save South Korea, Kim Il Sung decided to attack.

That was why, for the second time in nine years, Douglas MacArthur was awakened from his sleep by a call to arms.

Four days after the Communists attacked, they had entered Seoul and were driving the broken South Korean Army before them. The ROKs, as the Republic of Korea's soldiers were called, were powerless to halt them. Even though the United Nations had called upon its members to come to the assistance of embattled South Korea, it did not seem that any of them could get to the peninsula in time to stop the Communists.

On that fourth day, however, General MacArthur flew to the battlefront. The general wished to see how he could best execute President Truman's orders to assist South Korea. As his personal airplane, the *Bataan,* climbed the cloudy, dripping skies over Tokyo, the general reached into his pocket. He pulled out his old corncob pipe, and settled back to smoke. His aides grinned. The old war-horse was back in harness!

Landing at Suwon, 20 miles south of Seoul, General MacArthur com-

A Korean refugee carrying his possessions on an A-frame.

mandeered a jeep and rode north to the front. Nearing Seoul, he saw towering clouds of smoke rising above the city. Over the capital itself lay a black pall, through which the dull red light of fires glowed. Soon the general heard the crash of bombs and the crump of enemy mortars. A mile south of the city, he came to a little hill. He climbed it to observe the scene.

Obviously, Seoul was falling. Just as obvious, the South Korean nation was crumbling. Flowing around both sides of MacArthur's hill was the backwash of defeat. Ragged columns of panting, terrified ROKs mingled with throngs of civilians, many of them bent beneath A-frames on which they had piled their belongings. No one murmured, not even the children cried, as the great refugee tide flowed silently away from the stricken capital. Here and there, General MacArthur could make out the bright red crosses on ambulances stuffed with wounded soldiers.

Once again Douglas MacArthur was looking upon the haggard face of defeat. And once again he was making his plans for victory. He immediately concluded that South Korea did not have the power to stop the enemy. Nor was American air and naval support enough. No, American ground troops had to be brought to Korea immediately. With these, General MacArthur hoped to slow down and eventually halt the North Korean rush down the peninsula. This would be his parry. Then, after he had halted the enemy, he would strike hard in their rear. That would be his thrust.

Taking his corncob from his mouth, the general knocked the ashes from it and returned to his jeep.

As MacArthur well knew, the first part of his strategy—holding the enemy—would be the hardest. This was because time was on Kim Il Sung's side. Moreover, General MacArthur had to be careful not to leave Japan undefended. The attack on South Korea could very well be a trick to draw American strength away from that country. Then Communist China would be able to take over Japan unopposed. Nevertheless, MacArthur had to take that risk. Upon his return to Tokyo he ordered one of his four pre-cious American divisions to fly to Korea immediately. This was the 24th Infantry Division, commanded by Major General William Dean, a veteran officer.

It was still raining when General Dean's spearhead—a bare 406 soldiers routed out of bed or rounded up in town—went roaring through the skies from Japan toward Pusan on July 1.

Pusan was the finest port in South Korea. It lay at the extreme southern tip of the peninsula. Because of this, it was the enemy's chief objective. If they could take it, then all of Korea would lie helpless under the Communist banner. Even the most anti-Communist member of the United Nations would hesitate to invade a unified and hostile Korea. So Pusan had to be held open as one last corner of South Korean independence. Almost as important, it was the only modern port through which MacArthur could build his forces.

That was why the 24th Division's spearhead went rolling up the road from Pusan to Seoul. Its mission was to delay the enemy's advance south until more American forces could be fed into the battle. On July 5, the Americans met the oncoming North Koreans at a place called Osan. They were defeated. The Communists had too many tanks and too many soldiers. Moreover, many of the Americans broke and ran. Because they were mainly garrison troops, used to the soft life of the Japanese occupation, they were not mentally tough enough for the savage warfare fought in the stinking rice paddies of South Korea. Nevertheless, Osan made it plain that the United States was going to fight in Korea.

Meanwhile, General Dean got more of his 24th Division's soldiers into Korea. Again and again he formed them in defensive positions along the road from the north to Pusan. Again and again they were defeated. Yet, they were never crushed. After each setback, they turned to confront the North Koreans again, slowing them down a little more each time. They also got help from the Air Force and Marine and Navy aircraft flying from offshore carriers. Very quickly, the American fliers seized control of the skies and made it difficult for the enemy columns to advance. Over on the east coast, a second enemy advance was slowed down by ROK units supported from the sea by American warships.

As General Dean's weary and dirty soldiers fought on, growing in courage and battle prowess as they did, General MacArthur was rushing troops and supplies toward Pusan. In Japan, the 1st Cavalry Division was alerted to ship out. Back in the United States, the 1st Marine Brigade had taken ship and was tearing for Pusan at full speed. Until the reinforcements arrived, all depended on General Dean and his men.

On July 19, they made their last stand at Taejon, halfway between Seoul and Pusan. Two massive North Korean tank columns struck above the city, while a third smaller force came up on its undefended rear. Communist artillery rained shells upon Taejon, setting it afire. Halted at first, the North Koreans poured fresh reserves into the battle. At three o'clock the following morning, they cracked the American front. At daylight, the third enemy tank column came up through Taejon's open back door and burst into the burning city. That was the end of the battle.

East from blazing, roaring, exploding Taejon rolled the broken survivors of the 24th Division. General Dean was himself captured, and it appeared that the North Koreans' path to Pusan lay open.

But it did not. General Dean and his soldiers had fought long enough and hard enough to wreck the enemy's timetable. Their blood and agony had bought time—time for the 1st Cavalry Division to get to Korea, time for the 25th Infantry Division to follow. Gradually, the ROKs and the Americans formed a defensive ring around precious Pusan. Gone, now, was the enemy's chance for a lightning dash into the port city. Now, the soldiers of Kim Il Sung would have to blast their way in.

General MacArthur had now been appointed Supreme Commander of the United Nations Command in Korea. His forces included the U.S. Eighth Army, commanded by Lieutenant Gen-

Fresh American troops on their way to the front.

eral Walton Walker.

MacArthur chose Walker to defend Pusan. Walker was a veteran commander, having fought in both World Wars. The general was short and stocky. His uplifted jaw was suggestive of his bulldog spirit—just the quality needed to hang onto Pusan while MacArthur prepared to land far in the enemy's rear.

"Bulldog" Walker's first move was to draw his line of defense—the Pusan Perimeter—around the port city. The perimeter enclosed a rectangle about 80 miles long by 60 miles wide. To the right and rear it was protected by the sea. To its front and left it was held by men and arms along the line of the Naktong River flowing west from the coastal mountains and then turning due south.

Inside the Pusan Perimeter were two vital cities—Taegu, the provisional capital of Syngman Rhee's fugitive

161

Generals Walker (left) and Dean

government, and of course the port city itself. Both were now the objectives of the North Koreans. Either they would capture Taegu itself or sever the Taegu-Pusan road and thus isolate the two cities.

In late July, approximately a dozen North Korean divisions struck at Taegu from the north, and at the Taegu-Pusan road. Once again, they came on with tanks and behind heavy artillery barrages. They also unstrung the nerves of the Americans by launching "refugee attacks." Thousands of civilians, including women and children, were combed from the crowded roads and forced to march at gunpoint ahead of the North Korean soldiers. They were a shield of innocent, living flesh, and the Americans hesitated to fire into such helpless victims.

Sometimes also the North Koreans used spearheads formed of young South Koreans whom they had forced into their army. They hoped that by the time the UN troops had repelled the assaults of these involuntary soldiers, they would be out of ammunition. Then the North Korean regulars could go forward. Sometimes this happened, and the enemy broke through.

162

Against the tactics of an enemy who struck at him from every direction, "Bulldog" Walker had to become "Fire Chief" Walker. That is, he rushed his units from place to place, trying to put out the biggest enemy fires and hoping that the smaller ones would burn themselves out or be squelched by artillery or aerial bombing. It was a risky way of fighting, for it was possible that he might be rushing troops to the wrong place at the wrong time. Moreover, the alternating heat and rain of the Korean summer made the roads into dust bowls and quagmires by turns. Because the main thoroughfares were also constantly clogged with civilian refugees, military movement was often measured at a few miles an hour.

As Walker's tactics worked and his hard-pressed troops hung on, reinforcements and supplies continued to pour into Pusan. By August, big Pershing tanks at least the equal of the Communists' Soviet-built T-34s began arriving in Pusan. On August 2, the 1st Marine Brigade came into port. With this unit and three Army divisions, together with a reorganized ROK army, Walker's confidence rose.

But then the enemy crossed the Naktong River and threatened to take Miryang, midway on the vital Taegu-Pusan road.

Crisis had come within the Pusan Perimeter.

To drive the enemy from the Naktong Bulge and prevent them from cutting the Taegu-Pusan road, Walker called upon the 1st Marine Brigade.

With their own aircraft roaring low to bomb and strafe the enemy, the Marines attacked at a place called No-Name Ridge. Twice they were repulsed, but on the third try they drove the North Koreans back across the Naktong.

"The enemy was killed in such numbers," said the log of the carrier *Sicily,* "that the river was definitely discolored with blood."

That was the critical point of the Pusan phase of MacArthur's parry-and-thrust battle plan. It did not end the fighting immediately. Throughout August and during early September, the North Koreans hammered incessantly toward Pusan. This was their Great Naktong Offensive, employing some 98,000 soldiers in a series of thrusts against Walker's line. It was a poorly coordinated offensive. The North Koreans merely took all the roads and tried to slug down them into Pusan or Taegu. When they moved by day they were exposed to a dreadful scourging from the American air or, on the east coast, from both the sea and the sky. If they tried to escape aerial observation by attacking at night, they became disorganized in the dark.

By then also the United Nations Command outnumbered the North Koreans. Against General Kim Chaik's 98,000 men, Walker had 180,000 troops. Some 1,500 of these were the newly arrived British Brigade, 91,500 more were ROKs—and all the rest were Americans. This was more than

A scouting party watches for enemy movements across the Naktong River.

enough to hold off the North Koreans.

Still undaunted, the North Koreans continued to hammer at Pusan, completely unaware that General MacArthur was now ready to spring the trap behind them.

The parry had worked. The enemy had been halted and held. Now MacArthur was ready for the thrust. This was to be a landing nearly halfway up the Korean west coast at Inchon, the seaport for Seoul. If the Americans could land at Inchon and capture Seoul, they would cut off the North

Koreans at Pusan from their base. They would also catch the enemy between two fires.

MacArthur's plan was for the veteran 1st Marine Division to land at Inchon and capture Seoul. Then the 7th Infantry Division would land behind the Marines and wheel to its right to block all the supply roads south to Pusan. With its supplies cut off, the North Korean Army would have to face about north and try to fight its way out of the trap. When it did, Walker's force would pursue. This meant that the landing force in the north would become the anvil against which Walker, the hammer, would break the enemy into bits.

It was a brilliant plan, and also a very daring one. Almost at once, MacArthur received protests from the very Navy and Marine officers on whom he relied most for a successful landing. One of them said, "Make a list of landing 'don'ts,' and you have an extra description of the Inchon operation."

Chief among the "don'ts" were Inchon's massive tides. They were the second highest in the world, with an average 29-foot rise and fall of the sea. Some days the tide movement measured 36 feet, falling so fast that a boat might be stranded in ten minutes. Moreover, the tide action had built vast mudbanks running out from shore as far as three miles. This meant that the American landing ships could approach the shore only on days when the tide would rise at least 29 feet. There were only a few days a month when this would happen in daylight. Thus Inchon became the "first time in military history that the date of an invasion was dictated by the moon." Given September 15, October 11 or November 3 for his D-Day, MacArthur chose September 15.

Another "don't" was the narrowness of Flying Fish Channel, the entrance to Inchon Harbor. Ships would not be able to turn around in it, and might become sitting ducks for enemy coastal guns. Then there was Inchon's high seawall, which the Marines did

not like at all. Men climbing that seawall would be targets as visible as a fly climbing a windowpane. Almost as bad, the Marines would have only about an hour of daylight in which to take Inchon. This was because the high tide would not come until 5:30 P.M. and sunset was expected at 6:43 P.M. An hour and 13 minutes was not very much time in which to capture a strange, hostile port of some 250,000 persons, and then to prepare to defend it against nocturnal counterattack.

A third major handicap was little Wolmi-do, or Moontip Island. Wolmi lay in the harbor just west of Inchon, to which it was connected by a causeway. It was well fortified and it guarded all the approaches to the inner harbor. Its guns could strike at the Marines trying to storm the seawalls on both sides. Therefore Wolmi had to be bombarded into submission before the landings began. Yet, to strike at Wolmi before the invasion would be to forfeit the element of surprise on which General MacArthur counted so heavily.

Finally, no one could be sure of how the Communist Chinese would react to the landing. Would they allow their brother Communists in North Korea to be defeated? Of would they intervene, striking when a large American fleet jammed into a narrow harbor would be most vulnerable?

Such were the questions and objections raised when General MacArthur called his final council of war at his

165

headquarters in the Dai Ichi Palace in Tokyo. There were so many generals and admirals present in that big room that MacArthur called the meeting "a veritable constellation of silver stars." General J. Lawton Collins, the Army Chief of Staff, was present, along with Admiral Forrest Sherman, the Chief of Naval Operations. Thus, America's Number One Soldier and Number One Sailor had come from Washington to Tokyo to join in the arguments against the Inchon landing.

To General Collins, the landing at Inchon would be too deep in the enemy's rear. The invasion force might be cut off itself, and slaughtered. Instead of Inchon, Collins said, the landing should be made at Kunsan, much closer to Pusan and with few of the Inchon "don'ts."

Admiral Sherman seconded General Collins.

Rear Admiral James Doyle, commander of the invasion fleet, arose and said, "General, I have not been asked nor have I volunteered my opinion about this landing. If I were asked, however, the best I can say is that Inchon is not impossible."

A hush fell upon the room. All eyes were turned upon Douglas MacArthur, seated behind his desk, puffing on his corncob. MacArthur allowed the silence to turn into tension. His head was lifted as though he were still listening to someone. He was. It was the voice of his father, the hero of the Philippines, saying to him long ago, "Doug, councils of war breed

timidity and defeatism."

Then MacArthur began to speak. His voice was low, controlled. Sometimes, though, it rose in emotion. At other times, it sank to a dramatic whisper. Always he puffed his corncob, or jabbed it in the air to make his points. Twice he refilled it.

"The very arguments you have made," he said, "will tend to ensure for me the element of surprise. The enemy commander will reason that no one will be so brash as to make such an attempt. Surprise is the most vital element for success in war," he continued, beginning to speak of how Wolfe had surprised Montcalm at Quebec. "Like Wolfe," he said, "I will take them by surprise."

Addressing General Collins and Admiral Sherman, MacArthur explained that the proposed Kunsan landing would not work. It would not be deep enough in the enemy's rear to cut off his supplies. Better no amphibious hook at all than a short one. A jab, he suggested, was no substitute for a knockout punch.

"But seizure of Inchon and Seoul will cut the enemy's supply line and seal off the entire southern peninsula. . . . Without munitions and food they will soon be helpless and disorganized, and can easily be overpowered. . . .

"The only alternative to a stroke such as I propose will be the continuation of the savage sacrifice we are making at Pusan, with no hope of relief in sight. Are you content to let our

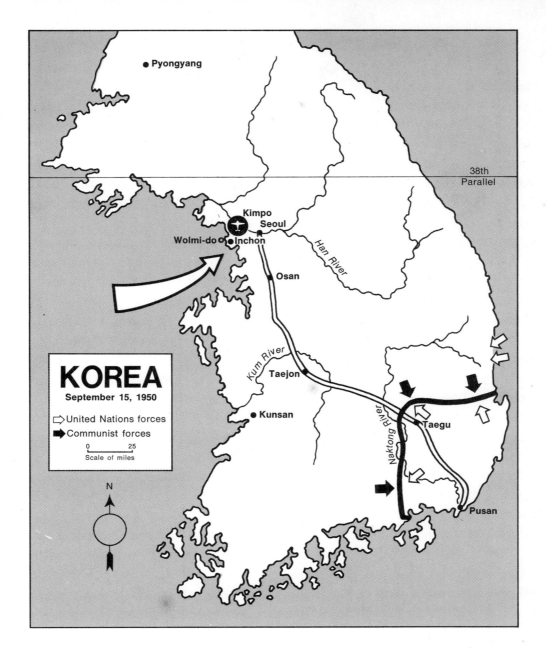

KOREA
September 15, 1950

▷ United Nations forces
◀ Communist forces

0   25
Scale of miles

N

troops stay in that bloody perimeter like beef cattle in the slaughterhouse? Who will take the responsibility for such a tragedy? Certainly, I will not!"

His voice sinking, General Mac-Arthur promised that if the enemy at Inchon proved too powerful he would withdraw his forces. "The only loss then will be my professional reputation," he said with a smile. Then he paused dramatically, and whispered,

"But Inchon will not fail. Inchon will succeed. And it will save a hundred thousand lives!"

Impressed, Collins and Sherman returned to Washington. Soon, Mac-Arthur received a directive from the Joint Chiefs of Staff which began:

"We concur . . ."

On September 13 Douglas Mac-Arthur boarded *Mount McKinley,* Admiral Doyle's flagship, in the Japanese harbor of Sasebo. Standing out to sea, *Mount McKinley* was struck almost at once by a typhoon. Wind and high water threatened to scatter and perhaps even wreck the American invasion fleet. Next day, however, the wind fell, the sea became calm—and a bright sun came out.

That evening, General MacArthur stood at the rail gazing at the sun sinking behind China over the horizon. He watched the waters of the Yellow Sea flash phosphorescent away from the ship's side. He thought with foreboding of all the risks of the morrow, when 40,000 Americans would risk their flesh at Inchon. For perhaps the first time, he allowed himself some doubts.

It grew dark. Steadily, stealthily, the great shapes of the ships slipped forward toward Flying Fish Channel. So much, the general knew, depended on surprise . . .

There came a flash across the water. A light winked on and off. MacArthur sighed. The channel navigation lights were on! He had surprised the enemy! Relaxed, Douglas MacArthur turned in.

The navigation lights seen by the Supreme Commander had not been left on carelessly by the enemy. They had been deliberately turned on by a brave naval lieutenant named Eugene Clark, who had scouted the harbor islands ahead of the invasion force.

Now, with the bombardment ships sliding through Flying Fish Channel, Lieutenant Clark sat shivering atop the lighthouse wrapped in a blanket. He watched as the transports carrying the Marine spearheads followed the bombardment ships. He would have smiled if he could have heard the Marine officer who saw the lights and whispered, "All the comforts of home."

It began to grow light. At 5:45 A.M. the naval guns swung in their turrets and began to spout flame and smoke. Assisted by British cruisers, the Americans pounded little Wolmi-do, the cork in the Inchon bottle. Next, blue Marine Corsairs roared low to bomb and strafe the beaches. Then, at 6:27, a battalion of Marines led by Lieutenant Colonel Robert Taplett went churning away for Wolmi.

Aboard *Mount McKinley,* Douglas MacArthur stood at the rail again, peering anxiously toward Wolmi, almost obscured by smoke.

Ashore on the vital little island, the Marines quickly overwhelmed its 500 dazed defenders. Soon tanks were landed to support them. Racing inland, the Americans raised the Stars and Stripes and threw up a roadblock on the causeway linking the island to Inchon. Forty-five minutes after the landing, Colonel Taplett radioed the fleet:

"WOLMI-DO SECURED."

A few minutes later an orderly handed the message to General MacArthur. His eyes shining, the general turned to Admiral Doyle and said: "Please send this message to the fleet: 'The Navy and the Marines have never

General Douglas MacArthur (in dark jacket) and staff members watch the invasion of Inchon from the bridge of his flagship, Mount McKinley.

shone more brightly than this morning.' Now, let's go down and have breakfast."

The surprise had been almost complete. By the time the tide went out, Wolmi was in American hands, and mounting American artillery. When the tide swept back in that evening, the Marines scaled Inchon's seawalls almost unopposed and drove into the city. That night, they braced for a counterattack. But none came, and in the morning they moved through Inchon's streets, followed by ROK Marines.

The following day, the U.S. Marines captured Kimpo Airfield in a tank battle, and that same day the 7th Infantry Division came ashore. While the Marines turned north to launch their fighting drive on Seoul, the soldiers wheeled south to block the North Korean escape routes.

Down at Pusan, the North Koreans were stunned to learn that the Americans were in their rear. Soon their supplies slowed to a trickle and then vanished completely. One by one the North Korean divisions broke off contact with Walker's units. They turned and raced north, hoping to get across the 38th Parallel before all the exits were slammed shut in their face.

It was then that Walker's ROKs and Americans, plus the British Brigade, burst out of the Pusan Perimeter in pursuit. The UN troops scourged the enemy all the way up the peninsula, aided once again by American air and sea power. Terrified and often leaderless, the North Korean Army broke into bits. Some divisions simply disappeared. Units surrendered en masse. Others merely melted into the mountains to conduct guerrilla warfare or practice banditry. And when an armored column from Pusan joined up with the 7th Division at Suwon, the rout of the cocky army which was supposed to win all Korea for Kim Il Sung was almost complete.

The North Koreans' only well-organized element was the garrison which was forcing the American Marines to pay dearly for Seoul. While the city burned around them, the Marines had to punch through street barricades covered by enemy machine guns and antitank guns. It was prob-

Marines scale the seawalls of Inchon.

Cleaning up Seoul. The Marines in the center are throwing hand grenades across an alley.

ably the fiercest single fight of the war. In the end, helped by ROKs and soldiers from the U.S. 7th Division, the Marines wrested the South Korean capital from the hands of the Communists.

On September 29, Douglas MacArthur flew to Kimpo Airfield. He had come to restore Seoul to President Syngman Rhee. All that he had dreamed, and more, had come to pass. At a single stroke he had broken and routed the enemy army that once was

so close to complete victory. The blue-and-white banner of the United Nations, the hope of free men everywhere, had risen triumphant above the red flag of slavery and despair.

As General MacArthur did not suspect on that joyful day, the fortunes of war were to change again. In less than two months, the Communist Chinese intervened on the North Korean side and a brand-new war was begun. It did not end for nearly two more years. But when it did, South Korea was still a free nation occupying a bet-

171

President Syngman Rhee (right) grasps General MacArthur's hand in gratitude for the liberation of Seoul.

ter defensive line just a little north of the 38th Parallel.

Thus, the Communist aggression eventually failed. And it failed chiefly because of MacArthur's daring parry and thrust. By this maneuver, the Communists were cleared from South Korea at an incredibly low loss of life, and they never came back to stay. By this maneuver, Douglas MacArthur thought as he drove toward Seoul, he had surely won the war.

President Syngman Rhee thought the same as he greeted the general in fire-gutted Government House. So did the UN Commission and MacArthur's top officers as they gathered under the broken skylight of the legislative chamber, to hear MacArthur declare with great emotion:

"By the grace of a merciful Providence, our forces fighting under the standard of that greatest hope and inspiration of mankind, the United Nations, have liberated this ancient capital of Korea."

MacArthur led the assembly through a recitation of the Lord's Prayer. Then he turned to Rhee and said, "Mr. President, my officers and I will now resume our military duties and leave you and your government to the discharge of civil responsibility."

The aged president seized the general's hand. "We admire you," he said, his faded old eyes filling with tears. "We love you as the savior of our people."

Index

175

About the Author

Reviewing Robert Leckie's most recent book for adults, *The Wars of America,* Allan Nevins calls him "a writer who, like Thucydides, knows how to get as much into one paragraph as most authors manage in a page."

Mr. Leckie has written nineteen books, most of them on military history, beginning with *Helmet for My Pillow.* This narrative of the author's experiences during World War II, in which he was wounded and decorated as a Marine in the South Pacific, won the annual award of the Marine Corps Combat Correspondent Association in 1957. A later book, *Strong Men Armed,* is a dramatic account of the great and relentless Marine drive across the Pacific from Guadalcanal to Okinawa. Robert Leckie's best-selling Landmark Books for young readers include *The Story of World War I, The Story of World War II, The Battle for Iwo Jima,* and *The War in Korea.*

Born in Philadelphia and raised in Rutherford, New Jersey, Mr. Leckie has had wide newspaper and film experience. He has worked on eight newspapers as a reporter, sports writer, financial editor, and copy editor. Formerly the editor of MGM's theater newsreel, he has also written documentary films and edited television news films. Mr. Leckie, his wife, and three children live in Mountain Lakes, New Jersey.